AF488109

Also by Eric Agyemang Duah

Mastering Courtroom Strategy with AI

The AI Uprising

The AI Messiah

The Memory Traders

Sworn not to Love Again

PERFECT PROMPTING

A Comprehensive Guide
for Professionals

Prompt Engineering Handbook

Eric Agyemang Duah

PromptTech
Consulting
and Publishing Services

Perfect Prompting: A Comprehensive Guide for Professionals

First edition: September 2024

ISBN: 9798227482174

**PromptTech
Consulting
and Publishing Services**

To Adom Nyame,
for granting me the wisdom, knowledge, and understanding
to write this book—
a work that has become a blessing to many.

"For the Lord gives wisdom; from his mouth come knowledge and
understanding."
—Proverbs 2:6 (NIV)

Contents

Preface

This book began with a question that resonates across professions: *How can we work intelligently with AI?*

As a generative AI professional and author navigating the accelerating pace of digital transformation, I've witnessed the urgent need for clear, practical, and ethically grounded guidance on leveraging large language models (LLMs) like ChatGPT, Gemini, Perplexity, and Copilot. These tools are not mere instruments of automation—they are potent collaborators in thought, creativity, and problem-solving.

That inquiry quickly led to *prompt engineering*—the essential craft for effective human–AI collaboration, shaping how professionals think, ask questions, and drive action.

Perfect Prompting: A Comprehensive Guide for Professionals is written for professionals, educators, students, and lifelong learners eager to harness AI's power while safeguarding the invaluable role of human expertise. This book is not a general celebration of AI; it is a structured, responsible guide to its most effective and ethical use.

The book is organized into four distinct and comprehensive parts: foundational AI concepts; core principles and techniques of prompting; practical use cases and tool integration; and extensive profession-specific prompt packs.

Whether you are a software engineer optimizing code, a teacher personalizing instruction, or an architect exploring generative design, I hope this guide offers the clarity and confidence to make AI work *with you*—not just for you, and certainly not around you.

Ultimately, this book reinforces the enduring truth: even amid intelligent machines, our progress is still defined by the quality of our questions, the clarity of our goals, and the strength of our values.

Eric Agyemang Duah
The Author

Introduction

The art of crafting effective prompts has become an indispensable skill for professionals across every discipline. In today's fast-paced, ever-evolving work environment, the ability to communicate clearly and concisely is not just beneficial, it is crucial for success. For any professional, whether a designer, writer, accountant, lawyer, software engineer, or marketer, the capacity to create well-crafted prompts is vital for the efficient and effective execution of job duties.

In this comprehensive guide, *"Perfect Prompting: A Comprehensive Guide for Professionals,"* we delve into the intricacies of crafting prompts that enable professionals to work independently and with minimal alteration. This book is designed to equip you with the skills and strategies necessary to create prompts that are clear, concise, and actionable, thereby streamlining your workflow and significantly enhancing your overall productivity.

As we embark on this journey of perfect prompting, it is essential to consider the broader landscape of artificial intelligence (AI). Understanding AI is increasingly critical for professionals seeking to enhance their effectiveness in a technology-driven world. We will explore several key subjects that illuminate the intersection of prompting and AI, including its definition, key elements, types, and its transformative impact on industries. We will also address the ethical and societal challenges that accompany AI, as well as how professionals across various fields can benefit from its integration into their workflows.

Throughout this book, we will explore the fundamental principles of effective prompting, including the importance of clarity, specificity, and relevance. We will examine various prompt types, such as task-oriented, problem-solving, creative, conversational, and analytical prompts, and provide practical examples of how to craft each one. Additionally, we will discuss common pitfalls to avoid and offer expert tips for refining your prompting skills.

The guide culminates in the final chapters with over 150 profession-specific prompt packs. This unmatched collection provides professionals across diverse industries with ready-to-use templates designed to drive productivity and seamlessly integrate tailored prompts into their workflows.

By mastering the art of perfect prompting, you can significantly improve your work quality, reduce errors, and increase your overall job satisfaction. Whether you are a seasoned professional or just starting out, this book provides the tools and knowledge necessary to excel and lead in your chosen field. Let us begin this journey of perfect prompting, and unlock the transformative power of effective communication in your professional life.

What is Artificial Intelligence?

Artificial Intelligence (AI) is a dynamic, rapidly evolving field that continually expands the capabilities of computer systems. Essentially, AI involves creating algorithms and models that enable machines to perform tasks that usually require human intelligence—such as reasoning, learning, problem-solving, perception, and decision-making[1].

Defining Artificial Intelligence

Artificial Intelligence can be defined as:

> *"The development of computer systems that can perform tasks that typically require human intelligence, such as understanding natural language, recognizing images, making decisions, and solving complex problems."*
> — *John McCarthy, 1956*

This seminal definition by John McCarthy, one of AI's founding fathers, remains relevant today despite the exponential growth in AI's scope and sophistication. Unlike traditional computer programs that follow fixed, rule-based instructions, AI systems process vast datasets, recognize complex patterns, and make informed decisions with minimal human intervention. These systems learn and improve over time, becoming more accurate and efficient as they encounter new information[2].

Eric Agyemang Duah

Mimicking Human Thought Processes

AI systems do not operate like the human brain, which relies on biological neurons. Instead, they use data structures, algorithms, and mathematical models to simulate aspects of human cognition. By learning from input data, drawing inferences, and applying logic or heuristics, AI can solve problems and often surpass human performance in speed, precision, and scalability. For example, AI diagnostic tools have demonstrated remarkable accuracy in detecting diseases from medical images[3].

However, it is important to note that AI lacks consciousness or emotional awareness. It does not "understand" in a human sense but generates outputs based on learned patterns and probabilities derived from training data[4].

The Evolution and Growth of AI

Since AI's inception in the mid-20th century, the field has evolved through distinct waves. Early research centered on symbolic logic and rule-based systems. Progress in machine learning introduced systems that recognize complex patterns and self-improve through experience. Today, deep learning—a sophisticated subset of machine learning— powers many widely used AI applications, from voice assistants and facial recognition to autonomous vehicles and recommendation engines[5].

AI has matured from experimental laboratory technology into a central innovation driver across industries such as healthcare, finance, transportation, marketing, and education. The global surge in AI adoption reflects its practical applications, economic significance, and the substantial investments it attracts from governments and corporations worldwide.

This foundational understanding prepares the ground for deeper engagement with AI's technical workings and, critically, for mastering

Eric Agyemang Duah

prompt engineering—the essential skill that enables professionals to communicate effectively with AI systems to unlock their full potential.

Eric Agyemang Duah

Key Elements of AI

At the core of the remarkable advancements in Artificial Intelligence (AI) lie several foundational elements that enable machines to perform increasingly complex and context-aware tasks. These key components—Machine Learning, Natural Language Processing, Computer Vision, and Robotics—are not only technological pillars but also the engines driving AI's rapid integration into professional, industrial, and social domains.

Machine Learning: The Adaptive Foundation

Machine Learning (ML) is a core element of AI that enables machines to learn from data and improve their performance without explicit programming. ML uses statistical models and algorithms to detect patterns, draw inferences, and make decisions based on historical or real-time input[1].

There are three main types of machine learning:

- **Supervised learning:** The system is trained on labeled data, where each input corresponds to a known output (e.g., spam detection in email).

- **Unsupervised learning:** The system finds hidden structures and patterns in unlabeled data without predefined outcomes (e.g., customer segmentation).

- **Reinforcement learning:** An agent learns by interacting with its environment, receiving rewards or penalties to optimize its behavior over time (e.g., game-playing AIs or self-driving cars).

Machine learning powers many of the applications we interact with daily, from Netflix recommendations and predictive text to fraud detection and medical diagnosis.

Natural Language Processing: Bridging the Human-Machine Divide

Natural Language Processing (NLP) enables AI systems to understand, interpret, generate, and respond to human language in a meaningful way. This capability allows machines to engage in human-like dialogue, analyze sentiment, translate text, summarize content, and even write code[2].

Virtual assistants such as ChatGPT, Google Assistant, and Alexa rely on NLP to process voice or text queries and perform actions. Businesses use NLP-powered sentiment analysis to monitor customer feedback. Healthcare providers extract critical insights from clinical documentation through NLP techniques. NLP combines linguistics, deep learning, and computational algorithms to process language, accounting for grammar, context, semantics, and intent.

Computer Vision: Seeing the World Through AI's Eyes

Computer Vision gives machines the ability to perceive, interpret, and analyze visual inputs such as images and video. Leveraging convolutional neural networks (CNNs) and other advanced models, computer vision systems can recognize objects, classify images, detect faces, analyze medical scans, and guide autonomous vehicles[3].

This technology finds widespread use in:

- **Security**: facial recognition and surveillance systems.

- **Retail**: smart inventory management through shelf monitoring.

- **Healthcare**: early detection of diseases via radiographic image analysis.

Eric Agyemang Duah

By mimicking human visual perception, computer vision empowers machines to interact effectively with the physical world.

Robotics: Bringing AI to the Physical Realm

Robotics integrates AI with mechanical systems to create autonomous or semi-autonomous machines capable of performing real-world tasks. AI-equipped robots can navigate environments, manipulate objects, and respond to changing conditions without continuous human control[4].

In manufacturing, AI-driven robots handle assembly with precision. In healthcare, surgical robots assist in delicate procedures. In logistics, warehouse robots streamline inventory management and order fulfillment.

Modern robots utilize data from multiple sensors—such as cameras, LiDAR, gyroscopes, and tactile feedback—that AI algorithms process to interact intelligently with their surroundings.

Together, these key elements form the fundamental building blocks of modern AI. Combined, they enable systems that can learn, reason, see, speak, and act—redefining how professionals work and how businesses create value in the digital age.

Eric Agyemang Duah

Types of AI

In the ever-expanding realm of Artificial Intelligence, understanding the different categories of AI is essential for professionals seeking to harness its power responsibly and effectively. AI is commonly classified into three primary types based on capability and autonomy: Artificial Narrow Intelligence (ANI), Artificial General Intelligence (AGI), and Artificial Superintelligence (ASI). These classifications reflect an AI system's depth, flexibility, and ability to perform tasks beyond its original training.

Artificial Narrow Intelligence (ANI)

Artificial Narrow Intelligence, also known as Narrow AI or Weak AI, comprises systems designed to perform specific tasks with high efficiency and accuracy within defined constraints. These systems lack the breadth to generalize knowledge or reasoning across domains without explicit retraining or human intervention[1].

While ANI systems do not exhibit human-like comprehension or reasoning, they are remarkably proficient at their specialized functions and deeply embedded in today's industries and consumer technologies.

Popular examples include:

- **Large Language Models (LLMs):** Platforms like ChatGPT, Gemini, Microsoft Copilot, Perplexity, Meta's LLaMA, and DeepSeek generate human-like text based on prompts. Despite architectural differences, they execute a focused task — language processing.

- **Recommendation Systems:** Services such as Spotify and Amazon tailor user experiences based on historical and behavioral data.

Eric Agyemang Duah

- **Facial Recognition Software:** Tools like Apple Face ID, Clearview AI, and Amazon Rekognition identify individuals for authentication, surveillance, and law enforcement purposes.

- **Healthcare Diagnostic Tools:** Examples include Google DeepMind's AlphaFold for protein folding, IBM Watson Health, and Aidoc's medical imaging solutions aiding clinicians in diagnosis.

- **Fraud Detection Algorithms:** Financial platforms like Mastercard's Decision Intelligence, PayPal's fraud prevention engine, and Stripe Radar monitor transactions for anomalies in real time.

- **Voice Assistants:** Siri, Alexa, and Google Assistant respond to voice commands within limited, pre-scripted domains.

Narrow AI systems power many tasks professionals encounter daily, especially in customer service, diagnostics, content generation, and financial analysis. However, they do not possess independent reasoning, emotional understanding, or the ability to generalize outside their training scopes.

Artificial General Intelligence (AGI)

Artificial General Intelligence (AGI), sometimes called Strong AI or Full AI, represents an intelligence with human-like adaptability and comprehension across a wide range of tasks. AGI would perform any intellectual activity a human can, including reasoning, problem-solving, creativity, ethical judgment, and emotional understanding[1].

Unlike ANI, AGI systems would generalize knowledge from one domain to others, learn efficiently with minimal data, and self-improve without human input, embodying autonomous, context-aware intelligence.

Key AGI Characteristics include:

- **Cross-Domain Learning:** Acquire and apply knowledge seamlessly across multiple fields.

- **Abstraction and Reasoning:** Understand abstract ideas such as justice, fairness, and strategic planning.

- **Contextual Awareness:** Grasp situational nuances, cultural contexts, and social dynamics.

- **Creativity:** Generate novel concepts, solutions, and artistic works.

- **Emotional and Social Intelligence:** Interpret and respond effectively to human emotions.

- **Common-Sense Reasoning:** Understand everyday cause-effect, assumptions, and heuristics guiding typical behavior.

Potential Benefits of AGI

If developed ethically and safely, AGI could revolutionize numerous domains:

- **Accelerated Scientific Discovery:** Autonomously generate hypotheses, design experiments, and analyze data across medicine, climate science, and physics[2].

- **Personalized Education and Healthcare:** Provide tailored tutoring and adaptive treatment plans in real time[3].

- **Cross-Disciplinary Innovation:** Solve complex global challenges like pandemics, clean energy, and poverty reduction.

- **Human-AI Collaboration:** Augment creativity and strategy in policy, architecture, design, and literature.

- **Advanced Automation:** Enable full automation of nuanced cognitive labor requiring judgment and reasoning[4].

Current Status and Research Directions

Despite breakthroughs in LLMs and multimodal models, no AI system today qualifies as AGI. Tools like ChatGPT, Gemini, and Perplexity operate within narrow domains and lack generalized reasoning, autonomous learning, or true understanding[5].

Research on AGI focuses on:

- Multimodal learning (integrating text, images, audio, video)

- Meta-learning (learning how to learn)

- Self-supervised learning (reducing reliance on labeled data)

- Human-in-the-loop safety mechanisms (ensuring value alignment and control)

Predictions on AGI's arrival vary, with some expecting breakthroughs in coming decades while others urge caution due to safety, ethical, and governance concerns[6].

Artificial Superintelligence (ASI)

Artificial Superintelligence (ASI) denotes a hypothetical AI that surpasses human intelligence in all domains: logical reasoning, emotional intelligence, creativity, and decision-making[3]. ASI would rapidly self-improve, potentially exponentially outstripping human cognitive capacities.

Potential benefits of ASI include:

- Solving global issues like climate change, pandemics, and energy crises.

- Transforming science, economics, medicine, and education.

- Accelerating advancements in space exploration, biotechnology, and governance.

Yet, ASI also poses profound ethical and existential risks. Without alignment to human values, superintelligent systems might behave unpredictably or dangerously[4]. Currently theoretical, ASI motivates growing research in AI alignment and safety.

Summary Table 1.1: AI Categories

AI Type	Description	Current Status	Examples	Key Traits
Artificial Narrow Intelligence (ANI)	Specialized, task specific intelligence	Actively deployed	ChatGPT, Siri, Face ID, Netflix Recommender	Fast, domain-specific, non-adaptive
Artificial General Intelligence (AGI)	Broad, human-level cognitive abilities	Not yet achieved (theoretical)	N/A	Adaptable, cross-domain, human-level cognition
Artificial Superintelligence (ASI)	Intelligence surpassing humans in all areas	Entirely theoretical	N/A	Autonomous, self-improving, exponential intelligence

Conclusion

Understanding these AI categories is crucial for prompt engineers and professionals who interact daily with AI tools. Today's leading applications—like ChatGPT and Gemini—are sophisticated Narrow AI systems that simulate understanding without genuine comprehension. Recognizing the differences between ANI, AGI, and ASI helps users set realistic expectations and prepare for the evolving AI landscape.

As the field progresses, prompt engineering will continue to be essential—starting with mastering Narrow AI's current capabilities and expanding into enabling effective human-AI collaboration as more general intelligence emerges. Ethical foresight, safety alignment, and sound governance will be vital to guiding AI's future impact responsibly.

Transforming Industries with AI

Artificial Intelligence is no longer a peripheral innovation; it has become a core transformative force across nearly every sector of the global economy. As AI matures, it enables professionals and organizations to reimagine workflows, improve decision-making, enhance efficiency, and create new forms of value. Whether in medicine, finance, education, manufacturing, or media, AI is being woven into the very fabric of how modern industries operate and evolve[1].

Healthcare

In healthcare, AI is driving a fundamental shift from reactive treatment to proactive, data-driven care. AI-powered diagnostic systems can analyze medical images such as X-rays, MRIs, and dermatological scans with precision rivaling and, in some cases, surpassing that of trained specialists. These systems detect conditions like cancer, fractures, or cardiovascular abnormalities in seconds, significantly reducing the time between diagnosis and intervention[2].

Beyond diagnostics, AI revolutionizes clinical decision support by predicting patient outcomes and suggesting treatment pathways based on patterns found in electronic health records. In operating rooms, AI-assisted surgical robots improve human precision, making minimally invasive procedures safer and more accurate. Additionally, natural language processing tools streamline documentation by transcribing physician notes, extracting clinical terms, and organizing patient records automatically. Drug discovery, once a time-intensive and costly process, is now accelerated by AI algorithms that analyze molecular interactions and propose promising compounds for further study.

Eric Agyemang Duah

Finance

The finance industry has long relied on data and predictive models. However, AI has dramatically enhanced the scale and sophistication of these capabilities. AI is embedded deeply in fraud detection systems, monitoring transactions in real time and flagging anomalies that may indicate fraudulent behavior. These systems learn from past activity, adapting continuously to new patterns and attack vectors[3].

Investment firms use AI for algorithmic trading, where complex models make split-second buying or selling decisions based on real-time market data. These decisions often surpass those made by human traders in speed and insight. In personal finance, banks and fintech platforms use AI to provide intelligent customer support through chatbots and assess creditworthiness by analyzing alternative data sources. Furthermore, AI-driven risk analysis tools help financial institutions comply with regulatory frameworks and manage exposure in volatile markets.

Education

AI is transforming education by personalizing learning and optimizing academic operations. Intelligent tutoring systems use machine learning to adapt content in real time, matching a student's pace, strengths, and weaknesses. These platforms provide tailored assessments, instant feedback, and customized study recommendations, helping students progress more efficiently with greater engagement[4].

Teachers benefit from AI-powered automated grading systems that handle routine evaluations such as multiple-choice or short-answer tests, freeing time for meaningful student interaction. AI tools can identify students at risk of falling behind by analyzing engagement patterns, performance trends, and attendance records. Administrators also use AI to streamline tasks such as scheduling, enrollment, and course planning, making educational institutions more efficient and responsive.

Eric Agyemang Duah

Manufacturing and Supply Chain

In manufacturing, AI supports the transition toward smarter, more resilient production environments. Predictive maintenance systems use sensors embedded in machinery to detect anomalies and forecast mechanical failures before they happen. This approach minimizes unplanned downtime, reduces maintenance costs, and prolongs the life of critical equipment[5].

Computer vision systems monitor quality control in real time, detecting defects or irregularities that manual inspection could miss. In logistics and supply chain management, AI improves inventory forecasting by analyzing historical demand alongside seasonality, promotions, and market shifts. This ensures products are manufactured and delivered at the right time, in proper quantities, and with minimal waste. AI-integrated robotics further enhance automation by performing complex tasks with speed and precision in warehouses, assembly lines, and distribution centers.

Retail and E-Commerce

Retailers increasingly rely on AI to create personalized shopping experiences and optimize backend operations. Recommendation engines analyze user behavior, including clicks, purchases, and browsing history, and suggest products that fit individual preferences. This personalization boosts customer satisfaction, sales, and loyalty[6].

AI also supports dynamic pricing strategies where algorithms adjust prices in real time based on demand, competitor pricing, and inventory levels. Customer service benefits from AI-powered chatbots and virtual assistants that provide instant responses, handle returns, and guide customers through product catalogs. Behind the scenes, AI improves inventory management by forecasting stock needs more accurately and suggesting optimal replenishment schedules. Visual search tools allow consumers to upload photos and instantly receive product matches, bridging the gap between inspiration and purchase.

Eric Agyemang Duah

Transportation and Logistics

Transportation is undergoing a technological renaissance with AI at the center of advancements in safety, efficiency, and autonomy. Autonomous vehicles use AI algorithms to interpret data from cameras, LiDAR, and GPS, making decisions about acceleration, braking, and steering. These vehicles adapt to dynamic environments by predicting the behavior of pedestrians, traffic, and road conditions in real time[7].

AI also transforms logistics. Delivery companies employ intelligent routing systems that calculate the most efficient paths for trucks and couriers based on traffic data, weather, and customer availability. Predictive analytics enables anticipation of delays and proactive adjustments to ensure on-time delivery. In ports, airports, and distribution centers, AI coordinates human workers, autonomous vehicles, and robotic systems to streamline cargo handling.

Entertainment and Media

In entertainment, AI reshapes content creation, distribution, and consumption. Streaming platforms analyze viewing habits to recommend shows or music that align with user tastes. These systems continually learn from interactions to refine and personalize experiences[8].

AI also aids content creation. Music, scripts, artwork, and video clips are co-generated using AI models. Filmmakers use AI in post-production to automate editing, enhance visuals, and generate facial animations for dubbing. Journalism incorporates AI to produce news summaries, fact-check reports, and real-time data visualizations. Marketing teams leverage AI to analyze audience sentiment, optimize campaigns, and create hyper-targeted advertisements that resonate with viewers.

Conclusion

Artificial Intelligence is transforming entire industries by reimagining processes, empowering professionals, and unlocking new forms of efficiency and innovation. Its integration is not a matter of "if" but "how." Organizations and professionals that understand and embrace AI's potential will lead the way in shaping the future. As this transformation continues, it is critical that AI be developed and applied with strategic foresight, ethical consideration, and a commitment to enhancing human capability instead of replacing it.

Ethical and Societal Challenges in AI

As AI becomes increasingly integrated into decision-making systems, daily services, and organizational infrastructures, its societal implications grow more complex and urgent. While AI offers transformative potential, it also raises serious ethical concerns that professionals, developers, regulators, and users must confront. Understanding and addressing these challenges is essential to align AI's power with human values, rights, and dignity[1].

Bias and Discrimination

One of the most pressing ethical challenges in AI lies in bias—both in data and algorithm design. AI systems learn from historical data, and if that data contains biases—whether racial, gender-based, socioeconomic, or cultural—AI is likely to reproduce or amplify these biases in its outputs[2].

For example, AI-driven hiring tools have favored certain demographics due to biased training sets. Facial recognition technologies frequently show higher error rates for people with darker skin tones, reflecting imbalanced datasets. In the legal system, algorithmic risk assessments have disproportionately affected marginalized groups. These biases are not simply technical flaws but mirror human contexts in which AI is developed.

Prompt engineering can help mitigate bias by guiding models through carefully designed, domain-specific prompts. By refining prompts and training data, professionals can reduce unfair representations and promote fairness in AI decisions.

Privacy and Surveillance

AI's reliance on vast amounts of personal data raises significant privacy concerns. Whether for targeted advertising, personalized recommendations, or behavioral predictions, the collection and use of personal information present risks around consent, data ownership, and surveillance[3].

Governments and corporations increasingly deploy AI to monitor user behavior, collect biometric data, and analyze online activity. In some regions, AI-enabled surveillance systems track citizens' movements and interactions with minimal oversight, risking violations of civil liberties, social manipulation, and loss of autonomy.

Transparency and Explainability

Many AI systems, especially those based on deep learning, function as black boxes—producing results without clear explanations. This opacity is particularly problematic in critical domains such as healthcare, finance, and criminal justice, where stakeholders need to understand AI decision rationales[4].

Thoughtful prompt design can enhance transparency by instructing AI to provide explanations alongside its conclusions, empowering professionals to better understand, evaluate, and trust AI outputs.

Explainable AI (XAI) is an emerging field focused on increasing algorithm interpretability. Despite advances, a significant gap remains between technical complexity and end-user comprehension. Without transparency, trust erodes and accountability diminishes.

Job Insecurity and Economic Inequality

While AI is poised to create new roles, it will also automate many jobs, especially those involving routine or middle-skilled tasks. Sectors such as manufacturing, transportation, and customer service already face restructuring[5]. This shift risks widening economic inequality as high-skilled professionals gain from AI, while lower-skilled workers face job insecurity.

Professionals engaged in prompt engineering can help by creating AI solutions that augment human abilities rather than fully replacing workers, emphasizing collaboration and upskilling through prompt-augmented workflows.

Without robust reskilling initiatives, inclusive economic strategies, and social safety nets, AI could exacerbate income disparities.

Autonomy, Control, and Responsibility

As AI systems gain more autonomy, accountability questions become urgent. Who is responsible if an autonomous vehicle causes an accident, or when an AI denies a loan or parole? Responsibility often diffuses among developers, deployers, and users, creating legal and ethical gray areas[6].

In prompt engineering, crafting checkpoints and constraints within prompts can maintain human oversight within autonomous systems, preserving a layer of professional or regulatory control. Unexpected AI behaviors and opaque models compound this challenge. Establishing human-in-the-loop frameworks, clear liability guidelines, and ongoing monitoring is essential to ensure accountability.

Global Inequity and AI Access

AI development is concentrated in a few countries and corporations, while many developing nations struggle with infrastructure and resource barriers[7]. This imbalance risks deepening global divides, advancing progress for some regions while leaving others behind.

Inclusive prompt engineering practices—incorporating diverse datasets and perspectives—can help make AI more equitable and globally relevant, reducing cultural and language exclusion.

Eric Agyemang Duah

Additionally, AI trained mainly on dominant cultural or linguistic data may fail to serve diverse populations effectively, risking exclusion and cultural erasure.

Regulation and Governance

Legal frameworks struggle to keep pace with AI innovation, leaving unresolved questions around data protection, fairness, intellectual property, and accountability[8].

Efforts such as the EU's AI Act and UNESCO's AI ethics guidelines mark important progress. However, regulation must balance innovation and oversight and remain adaptable as AI evolves. Effective governance requires collaboration among policymakers, technologists, ethicists, and civil society.

AI Alignment and Long-Term Safety

Developing increasingly general or autonomous AI raises long-term safety concerns. AI systems not aligned with human values may pursue harmful or unintended goals. These risks arise not only from hypothetical superintelligence but from today's systems exhibiting unexpected behaviors due to flawed objectives or misinterpreted prompts[9].

Prompt engineering plays a foundational role in alignment: precise prompts help communicate human intent, guiding AI behavior toward outcomes consistent with ethical standards and professional values.

AI alignment research aims to create models that reason about human values, defer to preferences, and avoid manipulative conduct. As AI power grows, alignment becomes both a technical challenge and a moral imperative.

Eric Agyemang Duah

The Human Role in the AI Age

AI is ultimately a tool shaped by human values and intentions. Ensuring AI serves humanity requires ongoing reflection, cross-disciplinary dialogue, and active professional engagement. The paramount question is not only what AI *can* do, but what it *should* do—and who decides.

Conclusion

As AI continues to transform society profoundly, ethical awareness is no longer optional—it is a professional obligation. The true measure of progress will not be the intelligence of our machines, but the wisdom with which we deploy them. Whether designing systems, writing prompts, or adopting AI tools, every professional must help steer AI toward outcomes that uphold human dignity, equity, and justice. The future of AI is both technical and ethical; it must be human-centered by design.

PART 2

What is Prompt Engineering

Prompt engineering is the art and science of formulating inputs, called prompts, to guide an AI model in producing high-quality, relevant, and reliable outputs. It involves crafting clear instructions, setting the proper context, controlling tone or format, and iterating based on feedback. A well-engineered prompt serves as both a question and a framework, enabling the AI to interpret the user's intention more effectively[1].

In professional contexts, how prompts are designed directly influences the quality, depth, and direction of AI responses. Understanding the cognitive approach behind different prompt types allows professionals to engage AI as a thinking assistant rather than a mere tool.

Below are five core categories of prompts, each explained with use cases illustrating their roles in achieving diverse professional objectives.

1. Task-Oriented Prompts

Task-oriented prompts instruct the AI to perform a specific, clearly defined action, such as summarizing documents, generating emails, translating text, or rewriting content for clarity or tone. These prompts emphasize precision and structure, making them ideal for automating administrative, procedural, or textual tasks.

Eric Agyemang Duah

Example Prompt

"Draft a two-paragraph executive summary of the attached quarterly marketing report, highlighting performance metrics and campaign effectiveness. The summary should be written in a professional tone for internal stakeholders."

This prompt clearly defines the task, specifies tone, focuses on key content, and identifies the target audience. The AI is expected to extract and organize relevant insights while maintaining concise and coherent language. Task-oriented prompts are widely applicable in legal, medical, administrative, and communications roles, where precision and clarity are essential.

2. Creative Prompts

Creative prompts encourage the AI to generate original content, explore possibilities, or provide stylistic variety. They often involve open-ended thinking, imaginative scenarios, or persuasive language, supporting roles related to storytelling, branding, ideation, and audience engagement.

Example Prompt

"Write a short promotional script for a 30-second radio ad promoting a new eco-friendly electric bike brand. The tone should be exciting, youthful, and focused on sustainability."

This prompt directs the AI to create original content within clear stylistic constraints. The AI must employ persuasive language and emotional resonance to capture the listener's attention. Creative prompts empower marketers, copywriters, educators, and designers to quickly produce compelling narratives, slogans, or campaign material.

3. Problem-Solving Prompts

Problem-solving prompts guide the AI in analyzing specific challenges, identifying root causes, and proposing feasible solutions. These prompts frame real-world scenarios and require the AI to apply reasoning and step-by-step logic.

Example Prompt

"You are an operations consultant. A logistics company has seen a 22% increase in delayed deliveries over the past quarter. Analyze potential causes for the delays and propose three solutions that could improve delivery speed and reliability."

By establishing a professional context, specifying a problem, and defining a deliverable, this prompt encourages the AI to consider operational factors and recommend actionable interventions. Problem-solving prompts are valuable for professionals in strategy, operations, supply chain management, engineering, and IT who rely on diagnostic and analytical skills.

4. Conversational Prompts

Conversational prompts create a natural, interactive dialogue with the AI, simulating human conversations or providing role-based guidance. These are helpful for coaching, training, support simulation, and practicing interpersonal communication skills.

Example Prompt

"Act as a professional leadership coach. Begin a coaching conversation with a mid-level manager struggling to give constructive feedback to their team. Use a warm, inquisitive tone and ask thoughtful questions to help them reflect."

This prompt sets the AI's persona, audience, and tone. It elicits a conversational response aimed at reflection and insight, supporting HR, training, customer service, and communication development professionals by simulating real human interactions.

5. Analytical Prompts

Analytical prompts challenge the AI to critically evaluate complex information, synthesize perspectives, and provide judgments. They typically present data or competing views and request comparative analysis, synthesis, or recommendations.

> ***Example Prompt***
>
> *"Analyze the quarterly financial reports for the company and summarize the key performance indicators, potential risks, and recommendations for improving profitability. Include a comparison to industry benchmarks and discuss the factors influencing the company's financial performance."*

This prompt directs the AI to interpret structured data, identify trends, benchmark against peers, and offer insight-driven recommendations. Analytical prompts are important for finance, research, journalism, policy making, and business intelligence professionals who require rigorous evaluation and evidence-based insights.

Conclusion

Each prompt type represents a distinct form of cognitive engagement—directive, generative, logical, interpersonal, or evaluative. Professionals who align their objectives with the appropriate prompt style can leverage AI more effectively as a collaborator, accelerating ideation, analysis, and decision-making. Mastering these different approaches transforms prompt engineering from a mechanical task into a strategic advantage.

Eric Agyemang Duah

The Significance of Prompts in AI

Prompts are the initial inputs or instructions provided to AI systems—particularly large language models (LLMs)—that shape their outputs. They encapsulate a user's intent, context, tone, and objectives in natural language form. In this way, prompts serve as the crucial interface between human cognition and machine-generated reasoning. As AI integrates more deeply into professional and creative workflows, the design of effective prompts has emerged as a key factor influencing both the performance and reliability of intelligent systems.

This section examines why prompts matter not only technically but also practically, strategically, and ethically.

Guiding AI Systems

At their core, prompts direct the behavior of the AI model. They establish the task, define the scope of the response, and set the tone or format expected. A well-constructed prompt does more than issue a command; it shapes the manner in which the AI "approaches" the task, despite lacking true understanding.

In high-stakes contexts such as medical diagnosis, legal document review, or financial forecasting, vague or poorly constructed prompts can produce misleading or erroneous outputs. Conversely, clear and focused prompts help the model align more closely with human intent.

For example, the prompt:

"Generate a summary of this patient's lab results."

is open-ended and could be interpreted in many ways, introducing potential risk.

Eric Agyemang Duah

Compare this with the more precise prompt:

> *"As a medical assistant, summarize this blood panel for a primary care physician. Highlight abnormal values and suggest possible causes, using medical terminology appropriate for a clinical note."*

This second prompt clarifies the role, purpose, tone, and content priorities, anchoring the AI's output in a human-defined framework of meaning.

Enabling Diverse Applications

One of the remarkable strengths of AI models lies in their flexibility across domains. The same model can assist in writing code, generating marketing content, performing legal analysis, or tutoring a student—provided it is given an appropriate prompt.

Prompts take various forms—including task-oriented, creative, analytical, and conversational types—that guide AI behavior to suit different tasks and professional objectives. These categories, discussed in detail in the previous chapter, illustrate how prompt engineering enables AI systems to be applied effectively across a wide range of industries—from education and entertainment to policy and product development.

This versatility underscores the growing professional demand for prompt engineering skills: the ability to frame questions and tasks in ways that unlock AI's full potential.

Facilitating Human-AI Interaction

At their best, prompts do not simply generate answers; they foster a dialogue between human and machine. They operate as the interface through which human intention and machine response collaborate—allowing AI to assist, refine, extend, or accelerate human work.

This collaborative interaction is especially valuable in fields where human-AI partnership is increasingly common:

- In healthcare, clinicians use prompts to draft reports, summarize patients' conditions, or produce clinical notes—saving time while enhancing accuracy.

- In education, teachers prompt AI tutors to provide tailored exercises, feedback, or explanations adapted to individual student needs.

- In business, managers employ prompts to rehearse difficult conversations, gather preliminary research, or draft communications.

In each setting, the prompt mediates clarity, collaboration, and control. When carefully designed, it enables humans to maintain agency while benefiting from AI's scale, speed, and pattern recognition.

Enhancing AI Performance

Although much attention focuses on the complexity of AI models, it is crucial to recognize that even the most advanced systems are only as effective as the prompts they receive. The same model can produce outputs ranging from excellent to flawed, depending solely on how the task is framed.

Effective prompts reduce ambiguity, prevent hallucinations, and steer the AI toward contextually appropriate results. This is especially important in professional environments where AI-generated content directly influences decisions, communications, or publications.

For example, consider the prompt for journalism or corporate use:

"Write a news brief on the GDP growth rate for Q3."

This could generate a generic or inaccurate summary.

Eric Agyemang Duah

By contrast, a more detailed prompt:

> *"Draft a 150-word business news summary on the 2024 Q3 GDP growth data in the U.S., using verified figures from the Bureau of Economic Analysis. Include a comparison with the previous quarter and maintain an informative, neutral tone."*

specifies length, content source, comparison, and tone, greatly improving the output's quality.

Hence, well-crafted prompts act as performance multipliers—enhancing precision, trustworthiness, and efficiency.

Advancing AI Research

Prompts play a foundational role in AI research and evaluation. Researchers employ carefully constructed prompts to:

- Measure model reasoning capabilities, biases, and coherence.

- Investigate how linguistic variations influence outputs across contexts.

- Develop and test benchmarks for tasks such as zero-shot and few-shot learning.

Indeed, entire subfields—such as prompt-based learning and instruction tuning—focus on training or fine-tuning models based on structured prompt behavior.

Innovations in prompting strategies, including chain-of-thought prompting and self-reflective prompting, have revealed new ways to elicit improved reasoning, creativity, and transparency from large models.

As explored later in the book in the chapter on Advanced Prompting Techniques, methods such as zero-shot, few-shot, and chain-of-thought prompting represent important strategies both for practical AI use and for advancing AI research.

Thus, prompts are not only practical tools for using AI but also critical instruments for understanding and enhancing AI systems.

Eric Agyemang Duah

Key Elements of Perfect Prompts

Crafting an effective prompt is both a strategic and creative process—central to successful human-AI collaboration. Within the emerging field of prompt engineering, well-designed prompts function as clear instructions and structured frameworks. They enable artificial intelligence systems to interpret tasks precisely, produce relevant outputs, and maintain alignment with the user's intended goals and tone.

The quality of a prompt depends on a combination of linguistic, structural, and contextual features. A prompt must clearly communicate intent, define boundaries, and convey specific expectations. Whether the task involves analysis, writing, summarization, or dialogue, the following components are essential to ensure that AI responses are coherent, accurate, and professionally useful.

1. Specificity

A strong prompt should be explicit and unambiguous, clearly articulating the task, parameters, and expected outcome. The more concrete the prompt, the more likely the AI will return focused and precise results.

Example Prompt

Calculate the net present value (NPV) of a proposed investment project with a five-year lifespan. The project requires an initial investment of $250,000 and has a discount rate of 8%. The cash flow projections are: Year 1: $50,000; Year 2: $60,000; Year 3: $70,000; Year 4: $80,000; Year 5: $90,000.

This prompt is highly specific because it provides all the necessary financial details and parameters required for a targeted calculation, eliminating the need for the model to make assumptions. Such specificity is critical in quantitative fields like finance, where precision is paramount.

2. Clarity

Prompts should use straightforward, plain language and follow a logical order. Avoiding unnecessary jargon and ambiguous phrasing improves comprehension and reduces the likelihood of off-target responses.

> ***Example Prompt***
>
> *Develop a social media marketing campaign to promote a new line of eco-friendly cleaning products. Identify the target audience, key messages, and metrics for measuring campaign success.*

This prompt is clear because it uses plain language and a logical progression to define the task and its key components. This clarity helps the AI immediately grasp the scope and structure of the expected output, which is especially beneficial in fields like business and marketing where a structured plan is essential.

3. Relevance

Prompts must be directly linked to the purpose, audience, and desired outcome. They should define meaningful tasks that produce contextually appropriate outputs serving real professional or educational functions.

Eric Agyemang Duah

Example Prompt

Write a 1,000-word feature article for a business magazine profiling a successful entrepreneur who has disrupted their industry through innovative practices and sustainable business models.

This prompt is relevant as it is directly tied to a real-world scenario and a specific audience (*Readers of a business magazine*). This ensures the AI's output is not only accurate but also engaging and valuable within a professional publishing context.

4. Context

Effective prompts provide necessary background information, framing the scenario, constraints, audience, or purpose. Context enables the AI model to understand not only what to do but how and why.

Example Prompt

Design a user interface for a mobile banking app that prioritizes security, ease of use, and personalization. Consider the needs of a diverse user base, including tech-savvy millennials and older adults less familiar with mobile technology.

This prompt supplies detailed constraints and user requirements, such as the key design priorities and demographic considerations. Context is especially important in design, policy, healthcare, and service-oriented domains.

5. Conciseness

Prompts should be as brief as possible while still communicating all necessary information. Brevity reduces cognitive load, keeps the task manageable, and helps the AI focus on essential instructions.

Example Prompt

Develop a content marketing plan to position a B2B software company as a thought leader in its industry.

This prompt is concise yet comprehensive, clearly stating the objective without extraneous detail. Conciseness is particularly valuable in fast-paced professional environments requiring clarity and speed.

6. Consistency

When using multiple prompts—such as for a series of related tasks or content—consistency in tone, style, complexity, and formatting is critical. This ensures coherence across outputs and facilitates comparison.

> ***Example Prompt***
>
> *Write a series of blog posts exploring the impact of artificial intelligence on various industries, such as healthcare, finance, and transportation.*

This prompt frames a consistent structure and tone across the series, making it suitable for thematic campaigns or content collections. Consistency supports professional writing, education, technical documentation, and branding initiatives.

Conclusion

Crafting high-quality prompts is foundational to maximizing the value and reliability of AI systems. By incorporating these key elements—specificity, clarity, relevance, context, conciseness, and consistency—users can design prompts that deliver more accurate, meaningful, and task-appropriate responses.

In essence, perfect prompts are not only well-structured but also purposeful. They reflect the user's intent and guide the AI to act with clarity, creativity, and professional precision. As AI becomes increasingly embedded in our workflows, mastery of these principles will determine how effectively we communicate with, and through, intelligent systems.

Advanced Prompting Techniques

As AI language models continue to evolve in complexity and capability, so too must the ways in which professionals engage with them. While foundational prompt elements—such as clarity, specificity, and context—remain essential, more advanced strategies enable users to extract richer, more structured, and more accurate outputs from these models. These techniques are especially useful when addressing complex reasoning, ambiguous tasks, or iterative processes.

In this section, we examine three key prompting strategies: zero-shot prompting, few-shot prompting, and chain-of-thought prompting. Each method represents a distinct way to guide large language models based on the structure and amount of information included in the prompt.

1. Zero-Shot Prompting

Zero-shot prompting involves asking the AI to perform a task without providing any examples. The model generates responses based solely on the phrasing and structure of the prompt to interpret intent and produce an appropriate output[1].

Zero-shot prompts are best suited for simple, well-defined tasks commonly encountered in the training data. They enable rapid assessment of the model's generalization capabilities.

Example Prompt

Summarize the key differences between renewable and non-renewable energy sources in two paragraphs.

With no examples provided, the model relies entirely on its internalized patterns. This approach suits high-level tasks such as summarizing, translating, or listing, particularly when brevity is required.

Zero-shot prompting is efficient for time-sensitive situations like generating quick insights, drafting outlines, or answering direct questions.

2. Few-Shot Prompting

Few-shot prompting provides the AI with one or more examples of the desired input-output format within the prompt. This helps the model infer the expected structure, tone, and reasoning[1].

Few-shot prompting is particularly helpful for nuanced or unfamiliar tasks where the format or domain specificity is critical.

> ***Example Prompt:***
>
> *Generate a customer support reply based on the following example.*
>
> ***Example 1 – Input:***
>
> *"My package hasn't arrived and it's been over a week."*
>
> ***Example 1 – Output:***
>
> *"We're sorry to hear your package is delayed. Please send us your order number so we can look into this right away."*
>
> **Now write a reply to this message:**
>
> *"I was charged twice for the same order."*

The model uses the example to replicate an empathetic, concise, and helpful tone. This technique is especially valuable in customer service, content moderation, UX writing, and technical documentation roles, where consistency in tone and format is essential.

3. Chain-of-Thought Prompting

Chain-of-thought prompting encourages the model to articulate reasoning through a sequence of steps instead of directly providing the final answer[3].

This method is well suited for complex, multi-step reasoning, problem-solving, or decision-making tasks requiring transparency in how conclusions are reached[3].

> ### Example Prompt
>
> *A student is planning to study three subjects: math, history, and biology. They have 5 hours and want to spend twice as much time on math as on history. They want to spend 1 hour more on biology than on history. How should they allocate their time? Explain your reasoning step by step.*

Rather than just producing the answer, the AI is expected to show its logical process—defining variables, forming equations, solving them, and interpreting the result. This enhances the clarity and verifiability of the output.

Chain-of-thought prompting is indispensable in analytical domains such as finance, policy analysis, engineering, education, and research, where rigorous reasoning and explanation are crucial[3].

Table 1.2: Summary Table of advanced prompting techniques and their unique function in professional practice

Strategy	Best Used For	Advantage
Zero-Shot Prompting	Simple, direct tasks with no provided examples	Fast deployment with minimal setup
Few-Shot Prompting	Domain-specific or format-sensitive tasks	Improves precision and consistency
Chain-of-Thought	Complex reasoning or multi-step problem solving	Enhance explainability and depth of analysis

By mastering these prompting techniques, professionals transition from passive users to active collaborators. These strategies empower users not only to obtain answers but also to shape the quality of AI outputs, aligning them with real-world objectives and standards of excellence.

Eric Agyemang Duah

Iterative Prompting and Prompt Chaining

Building on the foundational principles of specificity, clarity, conciseness, and context, as well as the advanced techniques of zero-shot, few-shot, and chain-of-thought prompting, we now examine further refinements. Iterative prompting and prompt chaining represent the next stage in this progression, designed to enhance user control, improve accuracy, and better simulate professional reasoning. These techniques facilitate dynamic, multi-turn interactions with AI, allowing for continuous refinement and complex problem-solving. Ideal for environments requiring detailed drafting, analysis, or instruction, they transform AI from a tool for single queries into an active collaborator within sophisticated workflows.

Iterative Prompting

Iterative prompting is the process of refining a prompt based on the quality of the AI's initial output. Rather than expecting a perfect response from a single query, iterative prompting treats the AI interaction as a dialogue. The user reviews the initial response, identifies areas for enhancement, and then adjusts the prompt accordingly. This re-prompting cycle continues until the output meets professional standards.

In professional contexts, where tone, accuracy, and detail are paramount, iterative prompting is essential. The following examples illustrate its importance across varied industries.

1. Report Drafting

Initial Prompt
Write a report on the impact of remote work on productivity.

AI Output
A general overview with minimal data, lacking structured sections and no cited studies.

Refined Prompt

Draft a 1,200-word professional report evaluating the impact of remote work on employee productivity in the tech industry. Include at least three recent studies, present key data points, and organize the content into an executive summary, key findings, and conclusion.

In corporate communications or consulting, clarity and credibility are paramount. By specifying audience, format, structure, and sources in the refined prompt, the user directs the AI to produce a professional, evidence-based report.

2. Data Interpretation

Initial Prompt
Explain this data table.

AI Output
A brief summary stating obvious patterns without interpretation.

Refined Prompt

Analyze the sales data in the table provided. Identify three major trends, offer possible explanations for each, and suggest two data-driven recommendations for improving Q3 sales. Present your findings in bullet points.

In business analysis and strategy, users require actionable insights. The refined prompt guides the AI to produce meaningful interpretation formatted for quick decision-making review.

3. Legal Research and Summarization

Initial Prompt
Summarize the key points of this court ruling.

AI Output
A vague list lacking legal terminology, jurisdictional details, or case implications.

Refined Prompt

Act as a legal research assistant. Summarize the Supreme Court's ruling in [Case Name], including the majority opinion, dissenting views, legal precedent cited, and implications for future constitutional law cases. Use formal legal language.

Legal professionals demand precise detail, terminology, and accuracy. Iterative refinement ensures content meets legal standards, supporting case briefs, writing, and academic analysis.

Conclusion
Iterative prompting allows users to treat AI as a collaborative partner — adjusting prompts to progressively approach the desired output. This mirrors how professionals write, edit, and revise in real-world workflows. Whether drafting reports, interpreting data, or analyzing legal judgments, iterative prompting ensures outputs meet industry expectations.

Prompt Chaining

Prompt chaining is the process of linking multiple prompts so that the output of one becomes the input for the next. This method enables users to complete multi-phase tasks, break down complex workflows, or simulate sequential reasoning. Instead of burdening a single prompt with multiple goals, prompt chaining distributes cognitive load across clear, structured stages.

The following examples demonstrate how prompt chaining streamlines workflows in document creation, multi-part analysis, and instructional design.

1. Document Generation

Prompt 1
Generate a bullet-point outline for a white paper on ethical challenges in AI deployment.

AI Output
A structured list of sections such as introduction, data bias, accountability, transparency.

Prompt 2
Using the outline above, write a 2,000-word white paper in a formal tone suitable for publication by a tech policy think tank. Include relevant citations and recommendations.

In professional writing, such as white papers or policy briefs, the process begins with logical structuring. Prompt chaining ensures foundational coherence before proceeding to content production.

2. Multi-Part Analysis

Prompt 1
List the major economic impacts of climate change in Sub-Saharan Africa.

AI Output
Bullet points highlighting GDP loss, agricultural decline, displacement, and more.

Eric Agyemang Duah

Prompt 2

Expand each point into a detailed analysis with statistics, causes, and potential policy responses.

Prompt 3

Summarize your findings in a three-paragraph policy recommendation brief addressed to the African Union.

Economists, policy advisors, and development consultants often progress from data gathering to deep analysis and finally stakeholder communication. Prompt chaining effectively maps this workflow.

3. Instructional Design

Prompt 1

Generate a learning objective for a high school course on digital citizenship.

AI Output

Students will be able to identify ethical and responsible online behaviour.

Prompt 2

Design a 3-lesson module to achieve this objective. Include titles, activities, and assessment methods.

Prompt 3

Create a 5-question quiz to assess student understanding after Lesson 1.

In education and instructional design, content must align tightly with learning objectives. Chaining prompts scaffolds the design process, assuring coherence and measurability.

Conclusion

Prompt chaining mirrors the natural professional tendency to decompose complex tasks into manageable steps. It facilitates refinement, deeper reasoning, and content reuse. Across publishing, education, and strategic analysis, chaining enhances coherence, control, and outcome quality.

Assigning Roles for Effective Prompting

In the evolving landscape of AI-human interaction, the skill of prompt engineering continues to grow in importance. Among the most powerful tools in a prompt engineer's arsenal is **role assignment**—the strategic technique of instructing AI to adopt a particular identity or persona. Whether conveyed subtly or explicitly, this method significantly enhances the contextual accuracy, tone, and relevance of AI-generated outputs.

This chapter explores three commonly used role assignment strategies: the **"Role"** technique, the **"Act as"** technique, and the **"Assume"** technique. Each enables the AI to respond from a specified perspective, aligning its output with professional expectations and real-world tasks. When used thoughtfully, role-based prompting transforms AI from a general-purpose assistant into a domain-specific collaborator.

1. The "Role" Technique

The "Role" technique allows users to assign a clear and professional identity to the AI model. This helps the model adopt the tone, focus, and depth associated with a particular expertise. Roles may be stated explicitly or embedded implicitly within the prompt.

Explicit Format Prompt Example:

> *"Role: Graphic Designer*
> *Create a sleek, modern logo design for a new sustainable fashion brand. Incorporate clean lines, a minimalist color palette, and a symbol that represents the brand's commitment to eco-friendly practices."*

Implicit Format Prompt Example:

> *"As a graphic designer, create a sleek, modern logo design for a new sustainable fashion brand. Incorporate clean lines, a minimalist color palette, and a symbol that represents the brand's commitment to eco-friendly practices."*

These formats guide the AI to adopt a designer's perspective, ensuring outputs reflect design principles, brand alignment, and visual storytelling. Explicit roles work well when clarity and instruction separation are necessary, while implicit roles offer a more fluid, conversational approach.

The "Role" technique is particularly effective for content requiring expertise and structured response. Whether explicit or implicit, role definition enhances precision and helps the AI deliver domain-relevant results.

2. The "Act As" Technique

The "Act as" technique directs the AI to fully embody a specific persona or character. This method excels in creative, performative, or persuasive contexts where domain tone and personality matter.

"Act as" Prompt Example 1: Film Director

> *"Act as a seasoned action film director. Provide a detailed breakdown of how you would choreograph and shoot a 5-minute car chase sequence for a high-stakes thriller, considering camera placement, stunt coordination, and post-production editing."*

This prompt instructs the AI to simulate a director's planning mindset, incorporating relevant terminology, cinematic techniques, and workflows.

"Act as" Prompt Example 2: ESL Teacher

"Act as an experienced ESL teacher working with adult immigrants. Develop a curriculum for a 10-week English language course that focuses on practical communication skills for the workplace."

This example shows the AI synthesizing educational principles, student needs, and curriculum design while maintaining a classroom-appropriate tone.

"Act as" is a versatile and immersive technique suitable for professional simulations, scenario creation, and tone replication. It is ideal for creative, instructional, or advisory contexts requiring depth and authenticity.

3. The "Assume" Technique

The "Assume" technique sets the scene by placing the AI in a specific situation or role, encouraging responses based on environmental, contextual, or hypothetical details. This method suits analytical, instructive, or scenario-based tasks.

The Assume Prompt Example 1: Copywriter

"Assume you are a copywriter. Create a sales page for a new e-book titled "Financial Freedom in 90 Days." The copy should be engaging, informative, and persuasive, highlighting the key benefits and features of the e-book to encourage readers to make a purchase."

This prompt frames marketing-specific tasks, guiding the AI towards persuasive language, product-focused formatting, and audience-targeted messaging.

The Assume Prompt Example 2: Pharmacist

"Assume you are a Pharmacist. Provide patient education on the proper disposal of unused or expired medications."

As a pharmacist, the AI uses accurate medical terminology and regulatory guidance while maintaining clarity appropriate for a patient audience.

The "Assume" technique is highly effective in scenario-based, client-facing, or regulatory contexts, generating realistic, context-sensitive outputs aligned with real-world environments.

Conclusion

Role assignment is a powerful enhancement to basic prompt engineering. Whether using *"Role:"*, *"Act as"*, or *"Assume"*, this technique gives the AI crucial context that improves accuracy, tone, and task relevance. It helps the AI generate content that mirrors human domain expertise, empowering users to unlock deeper and more credible professional outputs across virtually any industry.

Common Prompting Mistakes

Prompt engineering is essential for fostering effective and productive interactions between humans and AI systems, facilitating tailored and high-quality responses. However, crafting effective prompts presents many challenges. Professionals often make common errors, such as vague instructions, ambiguous wording, biased prompts, and contradictory elements, that compromise prompt effectiveness. These issues hinder the AI's ability to interpret user intent and generate desired outputs.

This chapter examines prevalent prompt crafting mistakes and offers proven strategies for overcoming them. By mastering these techniques, professionals, whether seasoned experts or newcomers in this dynamic field, can create clear, concise prompts aligned with their objectives.

Vague or Ambiguous Prompts

One of the most frequent mistakes in prompt crafting is vagueness or ambiguity. Such prompts lack clarity and often lead to inconsistent or irrelevant responses. To avoid this, ensure your prompts are specific, concise, and unambiguous. Provide clear instructions and define the desired output or task.

Example of a vague prompt

"Write a story about a person's day."

This prompt is vague because it lacks specific details about the person, setting, or focus. It leaves too much room for interpretation, risking responses that may not align with your intended purpose.

Example of a clear prompt

"Write a 300-word short story about a person's typical workday, focusing on the challenges they face and how they overcome them."

This prompt defines length, subject, and specific narrative elements, guiding the AI to generate a relevant and coherent story.

Overly Complicated or Long Prompts

While providing sufficient context is important, overly complex or lengthy prompts can overwhelm the AI and reduce output quality. Aim to balance detail with conciseness and focus.

Example of an overly complicated prompt:

Prompt

"Imagine you are a successful entrepreneur who has just launched a new tech startup. Your company has recently secured a significant round of funding, and you are now tasked with developing a comprehensive marketing strategy to promote your product and attract potential customers. Your strategy should include a detailed analysis of your target market, a multi-channel advertising campaign, and a plan for building a strong brand identity. Additionally, you should consider ways to leverage social media and influencer partnerships to amplify your message. The final deliverable should be a 10-page report outlining your proposed marketing strategy, including specific tactics, timelines, and key performance indicators."

This prompt combines excessive detail and multiple requirements, which may challenge the AI's ability to respond effectively.

Example of a more concise prompt

"Write a 2500-word marketing strategy for a new tech startup, including target market analysis, promotional tactics, and key performance indicators."

The concise version remains informative but focused, enabling the AI to generate a structured, comprehensive response.

Biased or Leading Prompts

Prompts should be phrased neutrally to avoid steering the AI toward a particular viewpoint or outcome. When prompts contain bias or assumptions—whether positive or negative—they can lead the AI to produce one-sided, unbalanced, or misleading responses. This reduces the value of the AI's output and risks misinforming the reader by ignoring important nuances or alternative perspectives.

Example of a biased prompt

"Write a positive review of the latest iPhone model, highlighting its superior features and design."

This prompt explicitly instructs the AI to focus only on favorable points, which may cause it to overlook or minimize any weaknesses or criticisms. The resulting output can lack balance and fail to represent a fair assessment.

Example of a neutral prompt

"Write a 500-word product review of the latest iPhone model, discussing its features, design, and performance in an objective manner."

This neutral prompt avoids leading the AI toward a specific opinion and instead encourages a balanced evaluation. The AI is more likely to produce an output that fairly covers both strengths and weaknesses, offering a comprehensive overview.

Lack of Contextual Information

Insufficient background or context makes it difficult for AI to generate relevant and coherent outputs. Ensure your prompts include necessary information such as setting, roles, or task context.

Example of a prompt lacking context

"Write a persuasive essay arguing for or against the use of renewable energy."

This prompt lacks context. Without context, the AI cannot tailor its arguments effectively.

Example of a prompt with sufficient context

"You are a policy advisor for a local government. Write a 1500-word persuasive essay arguing for the increased use of renewable energy sources in your city, addressing the environmental, economic, and social benefits of this transition."

This prompt provides clear guidance by specifying the AI's role *(policy advisor)*, its audience *(local government)*, the length of the essay *(1500 words)*, and the main topics to cover. This clear and detailed context helps the AI create a focused, meaningful, and relevant essay that meets the intended purpose.

Inconsistent or Contradictory Prompts

Make sure your prompts don't have conflicting instructions. Confusing directions can lead the AI to give unclear or mixed-up answers.

Example of an inconsistent prompt

"Write a 500-word creative story about a magical unicorn. The story should be factual and based on scientific research about unicorns."

This prompt is confusing because it asks for a creative story but also wants scientific facts about a mythical creature, which is not possible.

Example of a consistent prompt

"Write a 500-word creative story about a magical unicorn, describing its looks, powers, and the magical world it lives in."

This prompt fits the idea of a fantasy story and gives clear instructions, helping the AI create a clear and imaginative response.

Ignoring Tone or Style

Failing to specify tone or style can produce AI outputs that are too casual, overly formal, robotic, or mismatched with the context. In professional or sensitive settings, matching tone to audience and purpose is crucial.

Example of a prompt without tone guidance

"Write an article on mental health in the workplace."

This lacks tone and audience cues, risking an unfocused or inappropriate response.

Example of a prompt with clear tone and style

"Write a 700-word empathetic article for HR managers on supporting employees facing mental health challenges in the workplace."

The specified tone *(empathetic)*, audience *(HR managers)*, purpose *(supporting employees)*, and length *(700 words)*, enable the AI to tailor output appropriately.

Asking for Impossible or Unsupported Information

Prompts requesting speculative, future, or unverifiable information often lead to inaccurate or fabricated AI responses because such information lies beyond the AI's knowledge and reasoning capabilities. (For details on AI hallucination, see the *Limitation of Artificial Intelligence* section.)

> ### Example of an unsupported prompt
>
> *"Give a list of the top 10 stocks that will increase in value next year."*

Since AI cannot predict future market movements, this request risks generating made-up or misleading answers.

> ### Example of a supported prompt
>
> *"Summarize key factors financial analysts consider when predicting stock performance."*

This request focuses on established information and expert criteria, enabling the AI to provide reliable and informative content.

Conclusion

Prompt crafting is a deliberate, strategic process. Common mistakes, including vagueness, excessive complexity, bias, lack of context, and contradictions, can be avoided by careful wording, specificity, and clear framing.

A well-designed prompt serves as both a map and a mission. It directs the AI where to go and what to deliver. Applying these best practices enables professionals across industries to elevate the precision, relevance, and impact of AI-generated responses.

PART 3

AI Tools and Their Effective Use Cases

As explored in the preceding chapters, the effectiveness of AI-generated outputs depends significantly on how prompts are crafted. Equally important is understanding the platforms that receive these prompts. Each AI tool offers its own strengths, modalities, and interface features. Professionals must learn to navigate and leverage these tools to achieve maximum impact.

This chapter introduces some of the most widely used AI systems, which transform well-structured prompts into powerful professional outputs. From conversational assistants and multimodal generators to productivity enhancers and creative engines, these platforms enable users to draft, design, automate, and analyze more efficiently than ever before.

Whether you are building AI-integrated workflows or refining day-to-day content, mastering the tools featured here, such as ChatGPT, Gemini, Perplexity AI, and Microsoft Copilot, will deepen your ability to apply prompt engineering effectively in real-world contexts.

ChatGPT

ChatGPT, is a state-of-the-art conversational AI developed by OpenAI. It is designed to understand and generate text, images, audio, and code. It is widely adopted in education, software development, business communication, and creative writing. Its Pro version supports multimodal inputs, enabling users to analyze images, generate visuals and videos, write and debug code, browse the internet, and interpret uploaded files using an advanced code interpreter.

Features and Capabilities

ChatGPT handles complex reasoning, document analysis, DALL·E image generation, code writing, advanced data interpretation, and natural voice interaction. Pro users access priority response speed and enhanced memory. With Sora, users can generate high-quality video from text prompt, expanding the scope of AI-powered creativity.

How to Access ChatGPT

Visit ***www.chat.openai.com*** or use the mobile app. The free tier includes GPT-4o with basic tools. **ChatGPT Plus** ($20/month) and **Pro** (by invitation) unlock full access to advanced features, including Sora, file handling, and custom GPTs.

Gemini

Gemini is Google DeepMind's flagship multimodal AI model family. The latest Gemini 2.5 models include Flash, optimized for speed and efficiency, and Pro, designed for complex reasoning and long-context tasks. Both support native audio output, image and video generation, code creation, and extended memory. Gemini is used for content creation, research, technical analysis, and productivity enhancement within the Google ecosystem.

Features and Capabilities

Gemini supports multimodal interaction, document summarization, spreadsheet analysis, coding, and deep contextual understanding. It integrates seamlessly with Gmail, Docs, Drive, Android, and Google Cloud for enhanced productivity workflows. Gemini 2.5 introduced advanced image and video generation, audio synthesis, and real-time collaboration tools.

How to Access Gemini

Visit ***www.gemini.google.com*** and sign in with your Google account. The free tier includes Gemini 2.0 Flash. The AI Premium Plan ($19.99/month) unlocks Gemini 2.5 Pro, Flash, video capabilities, and app integrations.

Eric Agyemang Duah

Perplexity AI

Perplexity AI is an advanced conversational search and knowledge assistant that combines real-time web retrieval with powerful language models. It delivers concise, citation-backed responses, making it ideal for research, academic inquiry, and decision-making. Perplexity supports conversational queries and rich context-aware outputs. It integrates retrieval-augmented generation (RAG) to ensure factual accuracy.

Features and Capabilities

Models include GPT-4.1, Claude 3, Sonar, and Mistral. Features include document upload, live search, voice queries, multi-model chat, custom assistants, file analysis, image generation and shared collaboration Spaces. Perplexity Max enables unlimited Labs use, AI video generation via 'Ask Perplexity' on platform X, and agentic autonomous workflows.

How to Access Perplexity AI

Visit ***www.perplexity.ai*** and sign in with Google or Apple accounts. The free plan offers browsing and voice queries with GPT-3.5. The Pro plan ($20/month) includes advanced models, Labs, assistant creation, image and video generation, and enhanced multimodal tools.

Microsoft Copilot

Microsoft Copilot integrates AI capabilities directly into the core applications of the Microsoft 365 suite, such as Word, Excel, PowerPoint, Outlook, and Teams. This embedded functionality empowers users to automate document creation, derive insights from data, generate meeting summaries, and manage emails through natural language commands.

Features and Capabilities

Copilot supports natural language commands, document drafting, meeting recaps, spreadsheet insights, email composition, and slide creation. It includes Copilot Vision to interpret images and screens, voice-enabled workflows, screenshot analysis, and enterprise cross-application integration. Copilot Labs adds experimental tools for enhanced AI memory, reasoning, and interaction.

How to Access Microsoft Copilot

Visit ***www.copilot.microsoft.com*** or access through Microsoft 365 apps. Basic chat, voice, and image features are free. Copilot Pro ($20/month) adds GPT-4o and integration with Microsoft 365. Enterprise features require a Microsoft 365 Copilot license ($30/user/month).

Suno

Suno is an advanced AI music-generation platform that transforms text prompts into full-length songs with vocals and instrumentation, enabling users without musical background to create high-quality compositions.

Features and Capabilities

Powered by v4.5, Suno produces tracks up to eight minutes with vocal realism and emotional nuance. Stylistic editing tools like Personas and Covers, plus Remaster, Replace, and Fade Out, enable refined music creation. Real-time collaboration and audio remixing are supported.

How to Access Suno

Visit ***www.suno.com*** and sign up with a Google account. The free tier offers core functionality; the Pro plan ($8/month) grants access to v4.5, advanced editing, and commercial licenses.

Midjourney

Midjourney is a cutting-edge generative AI platform that transforms text prompts into high-resolution images and, more recently, experimental video and 3D visualizations. Built for artists, designers, and creative professionals, Midjourney fosters prompt-based visual storytelling with exceptional control and aesthetic precision.

Features and Capabilities

With its V7 alpha model, Midjourney introduces mood-board blending to combine visual themes, Patchwork canvases for collaborative storytelling, and advanced in-browser tools such as inpainting, outpainting, and zoom-based edits. It supports early-stage video and 3D output generation, expanding beyond static images. Users can access the platform via a modern web interface or the legacy Discord channel. Voice prompt input further enhances creative interaction.

How to Access Midjourney

Visit ***www.midjourney.com*** to subscribe. Plans range from $10/month (Basic) to $120/month (Mega), with commercial rights, web access, and GPU time varying by tier.

Eric Agyemang Duah

Canva AI / Magic Studio

Canva AI, housed within Magic Studio, is a powerful design assistant that empowers users to generate visuals, documents, and videos using natural language prompts. Designed for educators, marketers, and creatives, it accelerates creativity and streamlines workflows within a single interface.

Features and Capabilities:

Magic Studio includes tools like Magic Write for text generation, Magic Media for AI-created visuals, and Magic Design for layout suggestions. Users can edit images with Magic Edit, remove backgrounds, generate charts with Magic Sheets, and collaborate in real time. Voice prompting, animation, and basic video editing support diverse creative needs.

How to Access Canva AI

Visit **www.canva.com** and sign up for a free account. Some core tools are available at no cost; full access—including Magic Media, Sheets, Charts, AI Voice, Code, and unlimited Magic Studio features—requires a Pro subscription ($15/month).

Leonardo AI

Leonardo AI is a powerful generative image platform that enables creators, teams, and developers to generate high-quality visuals effortlessly. Its web-based interface offers full prompt customization, model fine-tuning, and an intuitive AI Canvas for sketch-to-art transformations, making it ideal for graphic design, concept art, and architectural visualizations.

Features and Capabilities

Powered by its Phoenix foundational model, Leonardo supports real-time editing through its AI Canvas and transparent PNG generation. The "Elements" and "Flow State" tools ensure visual consistency, while its 3D texture generator adds realism to game and architectural assets. Advanced capabilities include art and marketing bundles, animation-ready image-to-video output, and full API access for scalable creative workflows.

How to Access Leonardo AI

Visit ***www.leonardo.ai*** and sign up for a free account to receive daily image tokens. Paid plans start at Apprentice ($10/month) and scale up to Maestro Unlimited ($48/month), offering increased daily credits, commercial rights, API usage, and team collaboration features.

Cuebric

Cuebric is a browser-based AI platform that revolutionizes virtual production by generating cinematic environments in minutes rather than weeks. Designed for filmmakers, VFX artists, and production studios, it streamlines pre-production by transforming prompts and imported visuals into editable, camera-ready 2.5D scenes.

Features and Capabilities

Built on a Stable Diffusion backbone, Cuebric extracts depth and layers from 2D inputs through rotoscoping and AI inpainting. It produces photorealistic 4K-resolution sets, allows real-time composition adjustments, and exports depth-mapped environments directly to Unreal Engine or LED volume stages. Its partnership with Disguise enables live real-time shoot refinement, dramatically reducing production times and costs.

How to Access Cuebric

Visit **www.cuebric.com** to register. Cuebric offers tiered subscription plans for individuals and studios with options for 4K exports, depth segmentation, and Unreal Engine integration.

Eric Agyemang Duah

InVideo AI

InVideo AI is a web-based, text-to-video platform that streamlines the creation of complete videos—from script to final edit—using natural language prompts. Ideal for marketers, educators, and creators, it transforms ideas into polished multimedia content at scale.

Features and Capabilities

InVideo AI automatically drafts scripts, selects from a 16 million+ media library, generates humanlike or cloned voiceovers, adds subtitles and transitions, and applies dynamic virtual camera movements. Its AI-powered "Magic Box" allows prompt-based video editing such as scene deletion, voice accent modification, or visual adjustments without timeline complexity. Additional tools include voice cloning and real-time team collaboration.

How to Access InVideo

Visit ***www.invideo.io*** to sign up. The Free plan offers 10 minutes of weekly AI generation, limited media, and watermarked exports. Paid tiers—Plus ($28/month) and Max ($50/month)—add increased generation time, iStock assets, storage, watermark removal, and voice cloning.

Integrating AI into Workflows

Integrating AI into workflows positions prompt engineering as the bridge between human intention and machine capability. When prompts are used strategically, they convert repetitive tasks into intelligent processes that enhance speed, accuracy, creativity, and scalability.

This chapter presents a structured approach to integration, best practices for success, and practical use cases across industries. The focus is on moving from knowing most widely used AI systems to embedding them as reliable partners in daily operations.

Key Steps for Integrating AI Tools

1. Audit the Workflow

Identify tasks that are repetitive, time-intensive, or knowledge-specific. These are prime candidates for automation or augmentation. Examples include document drafting, image generation, summarization, video production, and structured communication.

2. Define the Role of Prompts

Clarify whether prompts will support ideation, automate content creation, enhance analysis, or produce visual or audio outputs.

3. Select the Right AI Tool

Match tools to tasks. Use ChatGPT for writing, Gemini or Perplexity for multimodal research, Leonardo, Canva AI, or Midjourney for image generation, and InVideo AI or Suno for media production. Selection should reflect task requirements, format compatibility, and access levels.

Eric Agyemang Duah

4. Create Modular Prompts

Design prompts that reflect the structure of the task. Break complex work into smaller stages: for instance, one prompt for outlining, another for refining tone, and a further prompt for summarizing or translating content.

5. Test, Refine, Repeat

Pilot prompts on a small scale. Refine their structure, tone, or clarity until outputs are consistent and reliable.

6. Integrate with Existing Platforms

Embed prompts directly into tools such as Microsoft Copilot in Word, Excel, or Teams. For ChatGPT or Perplexity AI, copy results into applications like PowerPoint, Google Docs, or content management systems.

7. Monitor Output and Feedback

Assess whether AI results meet professional standards. Document high-performing prompts and build a prompt library for team-wide consistency and efficiency.

Best Practices for Successful Integration

Integration is most effective when guided by structure and clear intent. Key best practices include:

- **Start small and scale gradually.** Begin with one or two workflows. For example, use Gemini to summarize meeting notes before progressing to automating an entire reporting process.

  Craft precise prompts. High-quality outputs depend on clear, role-specific, and context-rich prompts.

Eric Agyemang Duah

- **Maintain ethical boundaries.** Review AI-generated content carefully, particularly in sensitive fields such as legal, healthcare, or academia. Disclose AI assistance when required.

- **Keep humans in the loop.** Despite AI's capabilities, human oversight remains essential. Employ AI for content generation and ideation, reserving review, approval, and strategic decisions for human judgment.

- **Document and share workflows.** Maintain a repository of effective prompts and chains. Treat prompts as evolving templates that adapt to your team's changing needs.

Professional Use Cases

- **Marketing and Communications**
  Content teams can use ChatGPT to generate blog outlines and Leonardo AI or Midjourney to create corresponding header images. For video content, InVideo AI can produce short explainer videos based on these articles.

- **Education and Learning**
  Educators can employ Gemini to design curricula or quizzes, Canva AI to produce slides, and Suno to generate audio learning aids.

- **Visual and Product Design**
  Designers can develop mockups or branding concepts in Midjourney or Leonardo AI and refine layouts with Canva AI for consistency.

- **Corporate and Administrative Teams**
  Leaders can use Microsoft Copilot to summarize emails, generate Excel reports, and draft meeting notes. Integration streamlines communication and reporting.

- **Media and Creative Arts**
  Creators may combine Suno-generated music with Leonardo or Cuebric visuals, finalizing videos in InVideo AI for platforms such as YouTube or internal presentations.

Conclusion

Integrating AI into workflows is not about replacing human expertise but about amplifying creativity and efficiency through structured prompting. Whether drafting policies, developing campaigns, or designing multimedia assets, AI functions as a collaborative partner when guided by clear prompts and thoughtful workflow design.

Prompt engineering is the connective element between human intent and AI capability. Mastery of this skill allows professionals to transform everyday work into intelligent, scalable systems.

Eric Agyemang Duah

Limitations of AI

Artificial Intelligence (AI) offers powerful capabilities; however, its adoption necessitates a clear understanding of inherent constraints. Despite the remarkable outputs produced by tools such as ChatGPT, Gemini, Perplexity AI, and Midjourney, AI systems present technical, contextual, ethical, and operational limitations that may affect performance, reliability, and safety.

This chapter examines the most critical limitations of contemporary AI systems—particularly large language models (LLMs) and generative AI platforms—and proposes practical strategies to mitigate risks in prompt-driven workflows.

1. Lack of True Understanding

Although AI can generate text that simulates human reasoning, it lacks genuine comprehension of language. AI systems process input statistically, relying on training data patterns rather than true understanding or consciousness. Consequently, they exhibit limitations in:

- Grasping context beyond a fixed token window (context window limitations).

- Interpreting abstract, ironic, or culturally nuanced prompts.

- Maintaining coherence over extended, multi-turn conversations without topic drift.

Eric Agyemang Duah

Even advanced versions, such as ChatGPT Pro and Gemini Advanced, which provide extended context capabilities, fundamentally depend on surface-level pattern recognition rather than genuine cognitive depth.

2. Hallucinations and Misinformation

AI models may produce confident yet false or fabricated responses, commonly termed "hallucinations." These manifest as:

- Misquoting sources.

- Providing inaccurate statistics.

- Inventing legal or scientific claims.

This phenomenon is particularly problematic in sensitive domains such as healthcare, law, finance, and journalism. For example, Perplexity AI may cite ostensibly credible sources in real time but nonetheless produce inaccurate conclusions. Similarly, ChatGPT and Gemini can fabricate examples when queried for factual data.

Recommended Practice: Always fact-check AI outputs and treat generated responses as drafts or preliminary suggestions rather than definitive authorities.

3. Prompt Sensitivity

AI systems exhibit considerable sensitivity to prompt phrasing, where minor variations can produce significantly different outputs. Such unpredictability poses challenges in workflows that demand consistency. Examples include:

- Changing "Summarize the report" to "Can you summarize this report?" may result in alterations in tone or structure.

- Introducing ambiguity or multiple instructions within a single prompt often results in confusion or inconsistent responses.

Even experienced prompt engineers encounter inconsistencies unless prompts are precisely structured.

4. Bias and Ethical Risks

AI models inherit, and may amplify, biases embedded within their training data. Such biases encompass:

- Cultural or gender stereotypes.

- Political or racial biases.

- Reinforcement of exclusionary language.

These biases can subtly manifest in content generation, image creation, or decision-support tools, especially when prompts address issues of identity, ethics, or historical context.

Recommended Strategy: Employ inclusive and neutral language in prompts. Rigorously review outputs for unintended biases, particularly in public or client-facing contexts.

5. Limited Domain Expertise

While AI can imitate domain expertise, it lacks profound specialization. It performs optimally on general tasks such as summarization, brainstorming, and rephrasing. Limitations arise in:

- Complex legal reasoning.

- Advanced statistical analysis.

- Specialized scientific or technical documentation.

For instance, outputs such as code or financial models generated by ChatGPT typically necessitate review and refinement by domain experts.

6. Security and Privacy Concerns

Free and cloud-based AI tools may store or utilize user prompts for model improvement unless explicit privacy safeguards are established. Sensitive or regulated data—such as health records, client information, or proprietary research—should not be submitted to AI systems without a clear understanding of:

- Data storage policies.

- Data retention timelines.

- Compliance with relevant regulations (e.g., GDPR, HIPAA).

Recommended Practice: Use exclusively anonymized data with public AI tools or opt for enterprise-grade AI platforms that uphold stringent privacy protocols.

7. Dependence and Over-Automation

Excessive reliance on AI tools risks diminishing human critical thinking, creativity, and accountability. Prompt engineers must avoid delegating judgment-based tasks—such as ethical decision-making, hiring, or academic evaluation—to automated systems without appropriate human oversight. AI should augment, rather than replace, professional expertise.

Practical Prompt Packs
for Professionals

Building upon the foundational exploration of AI concepts, the anatomy of effective prompting, and advanced techniques such as zero-shot, few-shot, and chain-of-thought strategies, this chapter transitions from theoretical frameworks to practical application. It introduces structured, profession-specific *prompt packs* intended not merely as adaptable templates but as instructional tools that illuminate how large language models (LLMs) can actively enhance core professional functions.

Rather than offering static prompt examples, this chapter invites professionals to critically engage with the design of prompts tailored to their daily tasks. Through carefully curated scenarios across diverse disciplines, readers will learn how to align LLM capabilities with domain-specific challenges, optimizing outputs, reducing manual effort, and promoting innovation in areas such as decision-making, analysis, documentation, communication, and planning.

Crucially, the effective use of AI in professional contexts depends not on technical mastery alone, but on the application of sound judgment

Eric Agyemang Duah

and critical thinking. The ability to frame precise, context-aware prompts, to interrogate problems, evaluate outputs, and iterate responsibly, ultimately determines the quality and impact of AI-assisted work. In this sense, prompting is not merely a technical skill but a cognitive discipline that demands clarity, purpose, and domain insight.

By leveraging platforms such as ChatGPT, Gemini, Microsoft Copilot, Perplexity AI, and multimodal tools including Suno, Midjourney, Cuebric, Leonardo, and InVideo, the chapter demonstrates how AI systems can function as intelligent collaborators. Each profession-

specific section begins with a concise overview of the role, common pain points, and how LLMs can support or streamline specific tasks. This is followed by contextualized prompt scenarios that show not only *what to ask* AI, but *how to ask effectively*, emphasizing prompt design principles that are adaptable, transferable, and grounded in real-world professional needs.

Ultimately, these prompt packs serve a dual purpose: to expose professionals to the untapped value of LLMs in augmenting routine and strategic work, and to equip them with the critical prompting skills required to harness AI tools confidently and responsibly in their respective fields.

Accountants

The Essential Role of an Accountant

Accountants are vital in maintaining the financial integrity of individuals, businesses, and institutions. They prepare accurate reports, ensure regulatory compliance, manage audits, and provide strategic financial insights to guide decision-making.

Common Challenges Faced by Accountants

Accountants often face demanding reporting deadlines, the need to interpret evolving tax regulations, and the challenge of identifying inconsistencies in large financial datasets. Communicating technical findings to non-specialists and adapting to frequent changes in accounting standards also add complexity.

How AI Simplifies Accounting Tasks

AI tools, especially large language models (LLMs), streamline accounting tasks by generating summaries, analyzing regulations, detecting data anomalies, and drafting professional correspondence. These models enhance clarity, and increase efficiency across diverse financial operations.

Crafting Effective Prompts for Accounting Tasks

This section presents practical, role-specific prompts to help accountants and financial professionals leverage large language models (LLMs) like ChatGPT, Gemini, and Microsoft Copilot in their daily work. These examples are grounded in real-world accounting challenges, from drafting financial reports and forecasting cash flow to automating tax research and fraud detection analysis.

1. Financial Report Drafting

Scenario

An accountant needs to prepare a narrative summary for a quarterly financial report to present to the executive board.

Prompt

"You are a corporate financial reporter. Based on the attached financial data and key findings, draft a concise quarterly financial report. Include a clear executive summary highlighting the company's performance, a summary of key trends and KPIs, and a brief section on strategic insights for the next quarter."

How It Works

Using a tool like Gemini or ChatGPT, first, enter the prompt. Next, upload the raw financial data in a format like .csv or .xlsx, followed by a document containing your key findings from a .txt or .docx file. Then, submit. The AI will synthesize the information into a professional, narrative-driven report, saving significant time in the drafting process.

Eric Agyemang Duah

2.   Tax Code Research

Scenario

An accountant needs to quickly research a specific section of the tax code to determine how it applies to a client's unique financial situation.

Prompt

"You are a tax specialist. Based on the provided tax code excerpt and client scenario, explain the tax implications for [specify client type, e.g., a self-employed freelancer]. Simplify the explanation using plain, non-legal language and cite the relevant section of the code."

How It Works

Using a tool like ChatGPT, Perplexity AI, or Gemini, first, enter the prompt. Next, specify the client in the prompt entry, and paste the tax code excerpt and a brief description of the client's situation from a text-based file (.txt, .docx) directly below it, and submit. The AI will provide a simplified, well-researched answer.

3. Cash Flow Forecasting

Scenario

An accountant needs to create a three-month cash flow forecast for a small business to ensure it has enough liquidity to cover upcoming expenses.

Prompt

"You are a financial analyst. Based on the historical data and upcoming expenses provided below, generate a three-month cash flow forecast for a [specify business type]. Include inflows, outflows, and projected ending balances for each month. Identify any potential shortfalls."

How It Works

Using a tool like ChatGPT or Microsoft Copilot, first enter the prompt. Next, specify business type in the prompt entry, and paste the historical financial data and a list of upcoming expenses from a text-based file (.txt, .csv) directly below it, and submit. The AI will generate a detailed forecast to guide financial planning.

4. Fraud Detection Analysis Support

Scenario

An accountant is investigating irregularities in monthly transaction logs for potential fraud indicators.

Prompt

"You are a forensic accounting assistant. Based on the attached transaction data, identify unusual patterns and potential red flags for fraudulent activity. Analyze for anomalous transactions, duplicate payments, and unauthorized vendors. Draft a preliminary potential fraud report highlighting these findings."

How It Works

Using a tool like Gemini or ChatGPT, first, enter the prompt. Next, upload the transaction data in a format like .csv or .xlsx. Then, submit. The AI will act as an investigative partner, helping you find a "needle in a haystack" and accelerating the preliminary analysis.

5. Journal Entry Generation

Scenario

An accountant needs to generate a series of complex journal entries for transactions that are tedious to create manually.

Prompt

"You are a bookkeeper. For the transaction descriptions provided below, generate the corresponding journal entries. Include the date, account names, debit and credit amounts, and a brief description for each entry."

How It Works

Using a tool like ChatGPT or Microsoft Copilot, first enter the prompt. Next, paste the list of transactions from a text-based file (.txt, .docx) directly below it, and submit. The AI will generate accurate, well-formatted journal entries, saving time and reducing manual errors.

6. Expense Analysis with Visual Output

Scenario

An accountant needs to analyze a company's expenses for the last quarter to identify spending trends, pinpoint major cost drivers, and find opportunities for cost reduction. They require a visual output for management.

Prompt

"You are a financial analyst. Based on the expense data provided, perform an expense analysis for the last quarter. Categorize expenses, identify the top five spending areas, and highlight any unusual trends. Create a bar chart to visually represent the expense breakdown."

How It Works

Using a tool like Gemini or ChatGPT, first, enter the prompt. Next, upload the expense data in a format like .csv or .xlsx. Then, submit. The AI will analyze the data and generate both a written report and a visual chart for clear, actionable insights.

Architect

The Essential Role of an Architect

Architects design the built environment—residential, commercial, and civic spaces—by balancing functionality, aesthetics, safety, and sustainability. Their work shapes how people live and interact with their surroundings, making quality and precision fundamental to their profession.

Common Challenges Faced by Architects

Architects often struggle with iterative design revisions, managing client expectations, time-consuming documentation, and translating abstract ideas into visual concepts. Regulatory compliance and material specifications also add layers of complexity.

How AI Simplifies Architectural Tasks

AI—particularly large language models, can support architects by automating technical documentation, generating concept narratives, translating client briefs into spatial plans, and streamlining compliance research. It also enhances creative brainstorming through prompt-based design ideation and visual references.

Eric Agyemang Duah

Crafting Effective Prompts for Architectural Tasks

This section presents practical, role-specific prompts to help architects and designers leverage large language models (LLMs) like ChatGPT, Gemini, Perplexity, and multimodal tools like Midjourney and Leonardo AI in their daily work. These examples are grounded in real-world architectural challenges, from conceptual design and building code analysis to sustainable material selection and client communication.

1.   Schematic Design Generation

Scenario

An architect needs to quickly generate several conceptual design ideas for a residential project based on a client's brief, exploring different layouts and aesthetic approaches.

Prompt

"You are a design architect. Based on the client brief provided below, generate three distinct schematic design concepts for a residential home. Include a brief description of the layout, material palette, and the overall aesthetic for each concept."

How It Works

Using a tool like ChatGPT, Perplexity AI, or Gemini, first enter the prompt. Next, paste the client brief and project requirements from a text-based file (.txt, .docx) directly below it, and submit. The AI will provide creative starting points to explore various design possibilities.

2. Sustainable Material Selection

Scenario

An architect is designing an eco-friendly building and needs to select sustainable materials that meet specific project goals for a particular region.

Prompt

"You are a sustainability consultant. Based on the project requirements and regional context provided below, recommend three sustainable material options for the building envelope. For each option, include its environmental benefits, cost implications, and local availability."

How It Works

Using a tool like ChatGPT or Gemini, first enter the prompt. Next, paste the project requirements (e.g., building type, climate, budget) from a text-based file (.txt, .docx) directly below it, and submit. The AI will offer data-informed material recommendations to support your sustainable design goals.

3. Building Code and Zoning Analysis

Scenario

An architect needs to analyze a project brief against local building codes and zoning ordinances to identify potential compliance issues early in the design phase.

Prompt

"You are a code compliance specialist. Based on the building brief and zoning ordinance provided, identify any potential code and zoning issues for a [project type, e.g., multi-family residential building]. Highlight key sections of the code that require special attention."

How It Works

Using a tool like Gemini or ChatGPT, first enter the prompt specifying the project type in the prompt entry. Next, upload the project brief and relevant zoning ordinance document in a .pdf or .docx file. Then, submit. The AI will cross-reference the documents to provide a preliminary compliance report, saving significant research time.

4.   Sunlight and Shading Analysis

Scenario

An architect needs to perform a preliminary analysis of sunlight exposure and shading for a building design to optimize natural light and passive cooling.

Prompt

"You are a passive design analyst. Based on the geographical data and building orientation provided below, generate a report on sunlight exposure and shading for the building's façade throughout the day. Include visualizations of shadow patterns at key times (e.g., 9 AM, 12 PM, 3 PM) for both summer and winter."

How It Works

Using a tool like Gemini or Perplexity AI, first enter the prompt. Next, paste the location, building orientation, and design details from a text-based file (.txt, .docx) directly below it, and submit. The AI will analyze the data to provide an informed report and visual output.

5.   Construction Cost Estimation (Conceptual)

Scenario

An architect needs a quick, conceptual cost estimate for an early-stage project to help the client understand the potential budget before committing to a detailed design.

Prompt

"You are a construction cost estimator. Based on the project description provided below, generate a preliminary cost estimate. Include a breakdown by major building systems (e.g., structure, envelope, MEP) and provide a total estimated cost with a rationale for key cost drivers."

How It Works

Using a tool like ChatGPT or Gemini, first enter the prompt. Next, paste the project description from a text-based file (.txt, .docx) directly below it, and submit. The AI will provide a high-level cost estimate to guide your early-stage project discussions.

6. Creating 3D Architectural Visualizations from 2D Drawings

Scenario

An architect needs to quickly create a compelling 3D visualization of a project for a client presentation without the time and cost of a full rendering. They want to transform a 2D drawing into a realistic, immersive environment.

Prompt

"Generate a photorealistic 3D architectural visualization for the attached 2D building plan. Place the building in a [location/setting, e.g., a naturalistic, sunlit urban park] and create a scene suitable for a client pitch."

How It Works

Using a specialized tool like Midjourney or Leonardo AI, first enter the prompt specifying the setting in the prompt entry. Next, upload the 2D architectural drawing in a format like .jpeg or .png. Then, submit. The AI will transform your 2D design into an immersive 3D scene, providing a powerful and efficient way to visualize your project.

Author

Essential Role of an Author

Authors craft compelling stories, nonfiction works, scripts, and other written content to inform, entertain, or persuade audiences. They plan narratives, develop characters, conduct research, and refine language to convey ideas clearly and engagingly.

Common Challenges Faced by Authors

Authors often struggle with writer's block, maintaining consistency across drafts, structuring complex narratives, editing large manuscripts, and conducting timely research to support plots or arguments—all while meeting tight deadlines.

How AI Simplifies Authoring Tasks

AI tools like ChatGPT, Gemini, and Perplexity AI assist authors with brainstorming plots, generating character descriptions, summarizing research, rewriting drafts for clarity or tone, and automating formatting. These tools help authors accelerate their creative process, maintain stylistic consistency, and reduce time spent on repetitive writing tasks.

Crafting Effective Prompts for Authoring Tasks

This section offers hands-on prompts showing how authors can leverage AI tools like ChatGPT, Gemini, and Perplexity AI to overcome creative blocks, polish manuscripts, and accelerate the writing process. Each example features a realistic scenario, an optimized prompt, and a clear explanation of how the AI-generated output supports professional-quality writing.

1. Breaking Writer's Block with Plot Ideas

Scenario

An author struggles to continue a mystery novel set in Victorian London and needs fresh twists.

Prompt

"You are a novelist. Generate five original plot twists to revive a Victorian-era murder mystery, considering themes of betrayal, hidden identities, and societal scandal."

How It Works

Using a tool like ChatGPT or Gemini, enter the prompt and submit. The AI will deliver unique plot twists that spark creativity and help the author regain momentum, making progress on the stalled manuscript easier.

Eric Agyemang Duah

2. Drafting Compelling Character Backstories

Scenario

An author developing a historical romance needs vivid backstories for two protagonists to enrich emotional depth.

> **Prompt**
>
> *"You are a historical fiction author. Create detailed backstories (250 words each) for two protagonists in an 1850s coastal village: a widowed schoolteacher and a reclusive lighthouse keeper, including formative events, motivations, and internal conflicts that drive their choices."*

How It Works

Using a tool like ChatGPT or Gemini, enter the prompt and submit. The AI will produce rich, historically grounded character histories, helping authors establish authentic personalities and believable motivations. This depth enhances narrative cohesion and creates compelling arcs that keep readers engaged.

3. Enhancing Dialogue for Realism

Scenario

An author writing a contemporary thriller struggles to make tense conversations between a detective and suspect sound authentic.

Prompt

"You are a crime novelist. Rewrite the provided dialogue below to reflect a high-stakes interrogation between a seasoned detective and an evasive suspect. Maintain tension, realistic pacing, and psychological complexity."

How It Works

Using a tool like ChatGPT or Gemini, first enter the prompt. Next, paste your dialogue excerpt directly below it and submit. The AI will rework it with sharp, lifelike exchanges, ensuring characters speak naturally and interactions convey escalating stakes. This helps authors produce immersive scenes that grip readers and advance plots convincingly.

4. Professional Review for a Fiction Novel

Scenario

A novelist seeks an in-depth review of their completed fiction manuscript to evaluate character development, plot cohesion, and genre engagement.

Prompt

"You are a professional book reviewer. Read the attached fiction manuscript and craft a 1,000-word critical review discussing plot structure, pacing, character arcs, dialogue authenticity, and genre fit. Maintain a balanced, constructive perspective, identifying both strengths and areas for improvement."

How It Works

Using a tool like ChatGPT, Perplexity AI, or Gemini, first upload the manuscript in Word or PDF format. Next, enter the prompt and submit. The AI will provide a thorough, professional review, equipping authors with actionable insights to enhance storytelling quality and save the time and cost of a human critique.

5. Summarizing Research for Nonfiction Writing

Scenario
An author drafting a nonfiction book on climate change needs to condense a 40-page IPCC report into a digestible summary for a chapter.

Prompt
You are a nonfiction author. Summarize the key findings, statistics, and recommendations from the attached Intergovernmental Panel on Climate Change (IPCC) report in 1,000 words, highlighting points relevant to climate policy, adaptation strategies, and recent scientific updates."

How It Works
Using a tool like ChatGPT or Perplexity AI, first upload the IPCC report in PDF or Word format. Next, enter the prompt and submit. The AI will extract critical information and create a clear, chapter-ready summary, saving hours of manual reading and note-taking while ensuring no crucial details are overlooked.

6. Transforming Blog Series into a Cohesive Book Manuscript

Scenario

An author has written a 15-part blog series on mindfulness practices but needs help reorganizing it into a well-structured book.

Prompt

"You are a nonfiction author. Reorganize this 15-part blog series below into a cohesive 10-chapter manuscript with logical flow, engaging chapter titles, smooth transitions, and consistent tone. Provide a suggested table of contents."

How It Works

Using a tool like ChatGPT or Gemini, first enter the prompt. Next, paste the blog series text directly below the prompt and submit. The AI will restructure the fragmented posts into a polished manuscript with unified themes and professional organization, enabling authors to efficiently transform existing content into a publishable book.

Copywriter

Essential Role of a Copywriter

Copywriters craft persuasive, engaging content that drives action and conveys brand voice. From digital ads and product descriptions to website content and email campaigns, they transform ideas into words that sell, inform, or inspire. Their work supports marketing, sales, branding, and customer engagement across channels.

Common Challenges Faced by Copywriters

Copywriters often face tight deadlines, creative fatigue, and the need to tailor content for varied audiences and platforms. Maintaining originality while meeting client briefs and optimizing for SEO adds to the complexity of their role.

How AI Simplifies Copywriting Tasks

AI tools like ChatGPT, Gemini, and Perplexity AI support brainstorming, generate drafts, optimize headlines, adjust tone, and rewrite content for clarity or SEO. These capabilities boost productivity, spark creative direction, and allow copywriters to focus on refinement and strategy.

Crafting Effective Prompts for Copywriting Tasks

This section demonstrates how copywriters can leverage AI tools like ChatGPT, Gemini, and Perplexity AI to ideate, write, refine, and optimize marketing content across platforms. Each prompt features a real-world scenario, a strategically written prompt, and a clear explanation of how the AI tool delivers targeted, high-quality outputs aligned with copywriting objectives.

1. Writing an Attention-Grabbing Product Headline

Scenario

A copywriter is tasked with crafting a headline for a new eco-friendly detergent brand targeting environmentally conscious millennials.

Prompt

"You are a creative copywriter. Write five punchy, benefit-driven headline options for a new eco-friendly detergent brand targeting millennials. Highlight sustainability, effectiveness, and clean scent appeal."

How It Works

Using a tool like ChatGPT or Gemini, enter the prompt and submit. The AI instantly generates multiple headline variations with a tone, structure, and word choice tailored to resonate with the intended demographic and value proposition. This is ideal for quickly brainstorming and A/B testing.

2. Generating Website Copy for a Product Landing Page

Scenario

A freelance copywriter is developing website content for a startup that's launching a new AI-powered scheduling app designed for remote teams. The copy must be engaging, benefit-oriented, and optimized for conversions.

> ### *Prompt*
>
> *"You are a SaaS copywriter. Write compelling (150-word) landing page copy for a new AI-powered scheduling app designed for remote teams. Emphasize time-saving, integration with existing calendars, ease of use, and benefits for distributed teams."*

How It Works

Using a tool like ChatGPT or Gemini, enter the prompt and submit. The AI generates persuasive, structured landing page copy highlighting key features and emotional benefits. The output typically includes a headline, subheading, product benefits, and a clear call to action—all crafted to boost user engagement and drive sign-ups.

3. Writing a Series of Promotional Emails for a Product Launch

Scenario

A copywriter is hired to create an email sequence for the launch of a new online course teaching small business owners how to build an effective brand identity. The campaign needs to build anticipation, introduce the course, and drive conversions.

Prompt

"You are an experienced email marketing copywriter. Write a 3-part promotional email sequence for the launch of a new course titled 'Build Your Brand Blueprint.' Target busy small business owners. Each email should include a compelling subject line, engaging introduction, and persuasive call to action. Emphasize pain points, transformation, and urgency."

How It Works

Using a tool like ChatGPT, Perplexity AI, or Gemini, enter the prompt and submit. The AI will generate three distinct but connected emails, each tailored to guide readers through the awareness, interest, and decision phases. The result is a ready-to-use sequence designed to boost course sign-ups and engagement.

4. Crafting Product Descriptions for an E-Commerce Store

Scenario

A freelance copywriter is tasked with writing compelling product descriptions for a new collection of handcrafted leather bags, aimed at eco-conscious professionals shopping online.

> ### *Prompt*
>
> *"You are an e-commerce copywriter. Write three unique product descriptions (100–120 words each) for a line of handcrafted, eco-friendly leather bags targeting environmentally conscious professionals. Highlight sustainability, craftsmanship, functional design, and professional appeal. Each description should include an attention-grabbing headline, feature-benefit structure, and persuasive tone."*

How It Works

Using a tool like ChatGPT or Gemini, enter the prompt and submit. The AI returns three tailored product descriptions that balance vivid storytelling with strategic selling points. By aligning with the target audience's values and lifestyle, the output enhances product appeal, supports brand consistency, and increases the likelihood of conversion.

5. Repurposing Long-Form Content into Multi-Platform Snippets

Scenario

A copywriter wants to repurpose a 2,000-word blog post into multiple short-form content assets for digital channels.

> ### *Prompt*
>
> *"You are a content strategist. Repurpose the blog post below into:*
>
> *a 150-word LinkedIn post,*
>
> *a 70-word Instagram caption,*
>
> *a 60-word Facebook teaser, and*
>
> *a 30-word email preview.*
>
> *Maintain the original message but adapt each version for its respective platform's audience and tone."*
>
> [Paste blog post here]

How It Works

Using a tool like ChatGPT, Perplexity AI, or Gemini, first enter the prompt. Next, paste the full blog post directly below it and submit. The AI extracts key messages and reshapes them into format-specific, attention-grabbing snippets. This saves significant time and ensures content remains consistent yet customized for each digital platform.

6. Crafting Copy for a Limited-Time Offer Campaign

Scenario

A copywriter is preparing promotional content for an e-commerce store launching a 72-hour flash sale on eco-friendly kitchenware.

Prompt

"You are an e-commerce copywriter. Write compelling homepage banner copy (max 30 words), a 100-word promotional email, and a 60-word social media caption for a 72-hour flash sale on eco-friendly kitchenware. Emphasize urgency, sustainability, and the 40% discount, and use persuasive language tailored to environmentally conscious shoppers."

How It Works

Using a tool like ChatGPT, Gemini, or Microsoft Copilot, enter this multi-part prompt and submit. The AI generates channel-optimized marketing copy that aligns with the campaign's tone, urgency, and values. It helps copywriters efficiently create cohesive messaging across different platforms while preserving clarity and impact.

Designers

The Essential Role of a Designer

Designers transform ideas into compelling visuals that communicate messages effectively across print, digital, and product platforms. By blending creativity with functionality, they craft user-centered solutions that elevate brands and engage audiences.

Common Challenges Faced by Designers

Designers face hurdles aligning concepts to client expectations, tight deadlines, creative block, and repeated revisions. Balancing aesthetics with usability and clearly communicating design intent to non-design stakeholders are frequent obstacles.

How AI Simplifies Design Tasks

AI streamlines ideation by generating design variations, resizing assets, drafting social posts, and enhancing consistency. This accelerates workflows, freeing designers to focus on creativity while ensuring brand cohesion across deliverables.

Crafting Effective Prompts for Design Tasks

This section provides practical prompts tailored to help designers leverage AI tools like ChatGPT, Gemini, Midjourney, Canva AI, and Leonardo AI. These examples show how to generate fresh concepts, enhance branding, streamline visual production, and improve design communication. Each scenario includes a realistic use case, an optimized prompt, and a clear explanation of how AI supports creativity and efficiency.

1. Generating Logo Concepts

Scenario

A designer needs to generate initial logo concepts for a sustainable skincare brand.

Prompt

"Act as a creative director. Generate three minimalist logo concepts for an eco-friendly skincare brand, using earthy tones and nature-inspired elements. Provide a brief rationale for each concept."

How It Works

Using a tool like ChatGPT, Gemini, or Canva AI , enter the prompt and submit. The AI will generate minimalist logo ideas with explanations, accelerating ideation and providing designers with clear directions to develop concepts with clients.

2. Luxury Watch Ad Visual

Scenario

A creative team needs a sophisticated hero image for a luxury timepiece campaign.

Prompt

"Render a high-end wristwatch displayed on dark marble, illuminated by a dramatic spotlight to emphasize its brushed steel case. Incorporate subtle reflections to highlight craftsmanship, with a minimalist background for a refined, editorial look."

How It Works

Using a tool like Leonardo AI, Canva AI, or Gemini, enter the prompt and submit. The AI will produce   photorealistic visuals suitable for luxury advertising and editorial marketing materials.

Eric Agyemang Duah

3. Evening Gown Concept Sketch

Scenario

A fashion designer wants a glamorous sketch of a flowing evening gown for a couture collection proposal.

Prompt

"Illustrate a floor-length evening gown with a deep emerald satin fabric, plunging neckline, and delicate silver embroidery. Show the dress on a runway model, capturing movement and luxurious texture."

How It Works

Using a tool like Midjourney, Leonardo AI, Canva AI, or Gemini, enter the prompt and submit. The AI generates elegant fashion concept art, helping designers communicate design intent effectively to clients or stakeholders.

Eric Agyemang Duah

4.   Product Concept Render: Ergonomic Office Chair

Scenario

A product designer wants to visualize an ergonomic office chair concept for a new workspace furniture line.

Prompt

"Render an ergonomic office chair with breathable mesh, adjustable lumbar support, sleek black frame, and minimalist silhouette. Showcase the chair in a modern office environment with natural light and subtle background props."

How It Works

Using a tool like Leonardo AI, Canva AI, or Gemini, enter the prompt and submit. The AI produces photorealistic renders perfect for client presentations, marketing collateral, and design approvals.

Eric Agyemang Duah

5. Exploded View of Gadget Design

Scenario

A designer needs a clear exploded-view diagram of a compact portable blender for assembly instructions.

Prompt

"Create a detailed exploded-view illustration of a portable blender, showing motor base, blade assembly, detachable cup, and lid components, labeled clearly against a white background."

How It Works

Using a tool like Gemini, Canva AI, Midjourney, or Leonardo AI, enter the prompt and submit. The AI generates high-resolution exploded-view visuals optimized for user manuals, manufacturing documentation, or patent applications.

6. Textile Pattern Variations

Scenario

A fashion designer needs fresh patterns for a summer dress line targeting young adults.

Prompt

"Generate four seamless textile patterns featuring playful floral and geometric designs in a pastel color palette suitable for summer dresses, ensuring high-resolution and repeatability for fabric printing."

How It Works

Using a tool like Gemini, Canva AI, or Leonardo AI, first enter the prompt and submit. The AI will create editable, scalable textile pattern files ready for sampling, production, or mood boards.

Filmmakers

The Essential Role of a Filmmaker

Filmmakers orchestrate creative, technical, and logistical elements to transform scripts into compelling visual narratives. Their responsibilities span directing, cinematography, editing, and production management, uniting artistic vision with practical execution.

Common Challenges Faced by Filmmakers

Filmmakers often grapple with tight budgets, compressed timelines, creative blocks, and the need for meticulous previsualization. Managing large teams and coordinating complex shoots amplify these difficulties.

How AI Simplifies Filmmaking Tasks

AI tools streamline pre-production visualization, automate script breakdowns, and enhance editing. Cuebric AI assists with cinematic scene generation; InVideo creates storyboards or trailers from text; ChatGPT and Gemini draft scripts or refine dialogue, enabling filmmakers to ideate, plan, and execute projects faster with fewer resources.

Crafting Effective Prompts for Filmmaking Tasks

This section demonstrates how filmmakers can harness AI tools such as Cuebric, InVideo, ChatGPT, Canva AI, and Gemini to elevate every stage of production—from scriptwriting and visual development to editing and marketing materials. Each example prompt features a realistic scenario, an optimized request tailored to creative workflows, and a clear explanation of how AI streamlines complex filmmaking tasks, helping professionals translate ideas into polished visual content with greater speed and precision.

1. Tense Dialogue Exchange

Scenario

A screenwriter wants a fiery confrontation revealing secrets for a script.

Prompt

"You are an award-winning screenwriter. Write a 150-word heated argument between two rival homicide detectives in a precinct office, where one accuses the other of tampering with evidence to sabotage a case."

How It Works

Using a tool like ChatGPT or Gemini, first enter the prompt. Next, submit. The AI will produce a gripping, professionally crafted dialogue that emphasizes conflict and tension, ideal for screenplay development.

2. Crafting a Compelling Script Synopsis

Scenario

A screenwriter needs a gripping one-paragraph synopsis for a psychological thriller.

Prompt

"You are a professional screenwriter. Write a 150-word synopsis for a psychological thriller about a detective haunted by visions of his unsolved cases, exploring themes of guilt, obsession, and blurred reality."

How It Works

Using a tool like ChatGPT or Gemini, first enter the prompt and submit. The AI will generate a concise, suspenseful synopsis that captures the tone, stakes, and character dynamics, suited for pitching or funding applications.

3. Directing Scene Shot Lists

Scenario

A director needs to plan a tense, climactic courtroom scene and needs a thorough shot list for their cinematography team.

Prompt

"You are an experienced film director. Create a comprehensive shot list for a five-minute courtroom showdown scene where a defense attorney exposes a key witness's lies. Include suggested camera angles, lenses, lighting notes, and emotional beats to emphasize character reactions, shifting power dynamics, and tension-building moments."

How It Works

Using a tool like ChatGPT or Gemini, first enter the prompt. Next, submit. The AI will deliver an organized, professional-quality shot list that guides camera setups, visual storytelling, and mood shifts to ensure an impactful sequence.

Eric Agyemang Duah

4. Creating Cinematic Background Plates

Scenario
A filmmaker wants a photorealistic environment for a virtual production and needs a misty mountain range at sunrise to set an epic tone.

Prompt
"Generate a 2.5D cinematic background of a misty mountain range at sunrise with dramatic lighting, suitable for an epic fantasy film's opening scene."

How It Works
Using a tool like Cuebric AI, Invideo AI, or Midjourney, first enter the prompt. Next, submit. The AI will create a high-resolution 2.5D background with depth segmentation, ready for virtual production or Unreal Engine integration, enabling immersive environment visualization.

5. Previsualizing Action Sequences

Scenario

A filmmaker needs a storyboard for a complex car chase scene to communicate vision with the stunt team.

Prompt

"Generate a six-frame storyboard illustrating a nighttime city car chase with varied camera angles, including overhead shots, close-ups, and dynamic tracking perspectives."

How It Works

Using a tool like Cuebric AI, Gemini, or Canva AI, first enter the prompt. Next, submit. The AI will generate sequential cinematic storyboard frames showing key moments, camera placements, and movement directions to help plan stunts, pacing, and creative alignment.

6. Crafting a Social Media Trailer

Scenario

A director needs a 45-second teaser video to promote a new indie film on social media platforms like Instagram or TikTok.

Prompt

"Create a 45-second cinematic trailer for an indie romance film, using the following script excerpt below. Include upbeat music, dynamic transitions, and subtitle overlays."

How It Works

Using a tool like InVideo AI, first enter the prompt. Next,   paste your script excerpt from a text-based file (.txt, .docx) directly below it, and submit. The AI will automatically produce a polished teaser video with synchronized visuals, upbeat music, and text animations, which is ideal for social media campaigns.

Lawyers

The Essential Role of a Lawyer

Lawyers play a vital role in society by advising clients, representing them in disputes, and ensuring compliance with laws and regulations. Their work spans legal research, drafting contracts, negotiating settlements, and advocating in court. Effective lawyers protect client interests, uphold justice, and provide strategic guidance across civil, criminal, corporate, and specialized legal fields.

Common Challenges Faced by Lawyers

Lawyers often grapple with time-consuming document reviews, researching case law under tight deadlines, managing complex client communications, and keeping up with evolving legal precedents. Balancing workload with accuracy remains a key challenge.

How AI Simplifies Legal Tasks

AI tools like ChatGPT, Gemini, and Perplexity AI can automate contract analysis, streamline legal research, draft correspondence, and summarize lengthy documents, freeing lawyers to focus on strategy and client advocacy.

Crafting Effective Prompts for Legal Tasks

This section provides targeted prompts to help lawyers harness AI tools like ChatGPT, Gemini, and Perplexity AI in tasks such as contract review, legal research, drafting motions, and client communication. Each prompt includes a realistic scenario, an optimized prompt, and a clear explanation of how it works, enabling legal professionals to save time, improve accuracy, and deliver more effective counsel across diverse areas of practice.

1. Summarizing Complex Contracts

Scenario

A lawyer wants to quickly understand the key terms and potential risks in a 40-page commercial lease agreement.

Prompt

"You are a corporate lawyer. Summarize the attached commercial lease agreement in 300 words, highlighting critical clauses, tenant and landlord obligations, renewal terms, and any identified risks."

How It Works

Using a tool like ChatGPT or Gemini, first upload the contract in PDF or Word format. Next, enter the prompt and submit. The AI will extract essential contract details and generate a concise summary to facilitate faster comprehension and client advisement.

2. Drafting Demand Letters

Scenario

A lawyer needs to write a formal demand letter for unpaid invoices on behalf of a corporate client.

Prompt

"You are an experienced commercial litigation attorney. Using the provided contract details, draft a clear, assertive demand letter requesting payment of outstanding invoices totaling [insert amount]. Reference relevant contract terms, specify a payment deadline, and outline potential legal actions for continued nonpayment."

How It Works

Using a tool like ChatGPT or Gemini, first enter the prompt. Next, specify the amount involved, with contract details or correspondence summaries directly below it. Then, submit. The AI produces a polished demand letter with precise legal language to support effective debt recovery.

3. Conducting Case Law Research

Scenario

A lawyer preparing for trial needs a quick overview of recent rulings on non-compete agreements.

Prompt

"You are a legal research specialist. Provide a summary of the most recent case law on the enforceability of non-compete clauses in [insert jurisdiction], including key precedents, relevant statutes, and trends over the past five years."

How It Works

Using a tool like Perplexity AI or ChatGPT, first enter the prompt, explicitly specifying the relevant jurisdiction. Next, submit. The AI will scan authoritative legal databases and return a concise, up-to-date summary to aid in trial preparation.

4. Creating Customized NDAs

Scenario

A lawyer needs a non-disclosure agreement (NDA) tailored to a technology partnership involving sensitive intellectual property.

> **Prompt**
>
> *"You are a corporate attorney. Using provided project details, draft a tailored non-disclosure agreement for a partnership between a software developer and hardware manufacturer. Include clauses on confidentiality scope, permitted disclosures, duration, governing law, and breach remedies."*

How It Works

Using a tool like ChatGPT, Perplexity AI, or Gemini, first enter the prompt. Next, provide project specifics such as parties, purpose, and confidential information type directly below the prompt. Then, submit. The AI will generate a precise, legally compliant NDA draft protecting both parties' interests.

5. Motion to Dismiss International Trade Dispute

Scenario

A Ghanaian lawyer's client is being sued by a foreign company. The lawyer argues that the Ghanaian court does not have the authority to hear the case because the original contract requires all disputes to be settled through arbitration in Singapore.

> **Prompt**
>
> *"You are a Ghanaian commercial lawyer. Using the attached contract and statement of claim, draft a motion to dismiss for lack of jurisdiction. Cite the arbitration clause under Ghana's Alternative Dispute Resolution Act and relevant case law."*

How It Works

Using a tool like ChatGPT, Perplexity AI, or Gemini, first upload the contract and statement of claim in PDF or Word format. Next, enter the prompt and submit. The AI will draft a jurisdiction-based motion aligned with Ghanaian procedural law.

6. Preparing Deposition Questions in a Serious Fraud Case

Scenario

A lawyer representing a financial institution suspects that a senior manager has embezzled funds and needs a detailed deposition outline to uncover their role.

Prompt

"You are a white-collar crime attorney. Using the attached fraud investigation report and financial statements, draft 25 deposition questions covering fund transfers, suspicious transactions, falsified records, and potential co-conspirators."

How It Works

Using a tool like ChatGPT or Gemini, first upload relevant investigation reports and financial documents in PDF or Word format. Next, enter the prompt and submit. The AI reviews evidence and generates a logically structured deposition outline to aid the examination of key fraud issues.

Marketer

Essential Role of a Marketer

Marketers develop strategies to promote products, build brand awareness, engage audiences, and drive conversions. They research markets, craft messaging, create content, manage campaigns, and analyze performance data to optimize outcomes.

Common Challenges Faced by Marketers

Marketers often struggle to keep up with content demands across channels, personalize messaging at scale, interpret complex analytics, and maintain consistent branding. Time constraints and rapid market changes add further pressure.

How AI Simplifies Marketing Tasks

AI tools such as ChatGPT, Gemini, Perplexity AI, Invideo AI, and Canva AI help marketers automate content creation, generate personalized copy, A/B test headlines, analyze customer sentiment, and design visuals. These capabilities streamline workflows, improve targeting, and empower marketers to launch more effective, data-driven campaigns while freeing time for creative strategy.

Eric Agyemang Duah

Crafting Effective Prompts for Marketing Tasks

This section presents practical, role-specific prompts to help marketers and advertising professionals leverage large language models (LLMs) like ChatGPT, Gemini, Perplexity AI, and specialized tools like Canva AI and Invideo AI for daily tasks. These examples are grounded in real-world marketing challenges, from drafting compelling ad copy and creating social media strategies to generating engaging video content and advanced image editing for campaigns.

1. Integrated Script-to-Video Generation

Scenario

A marketer needs a complete teaser video for a product launch using prompt chaining on a single platform.

> **Prompt**
>
> *"Draft a 30-second teaser script for [product/event], highlighting unique features, emotional appeal, and a compelling call-to-action. Based on the script, generate a dynamic 30-second video, including energetic background music, branded text overlays, and fast-paced transitions for Instagram Reels and TikTok."*

How It Works

Using a tool like Invideo AI or Canva AI, with integrated video generation, first enter the prompt, specifying your product or event details. Next, submit. The AI will first create the script and then, using its video generation capabilities, produce a polished, professional marketing video efficiently.

Eric Agyemang Duah

2. Crafting Compelling Ad Copy

Scenario

A digital marketer needs to write concise and engaging ad copy for a new product launch across various platforms, ensuring it resonates with the target audience.

Prompt

"You are a seasoned copywriter. Draft three distinct ad copy variations for a new [insert product type, e.g., eco-friendly reusable coffee cup] targeting [insert target audience, e.g., environmentally conscious young urban professionals]. Each variation should be optimized for a different platform: Instagram (short & visual), Facebook (engaging & descriptive), and Google Ads (keyword-focused). Include a strong Call-to-Action (CTA) for each."

How It Works

Using a tool like ChatGPT, Gemini, or Microsoft Copilot, first enter the prompt. Next, specify the product type and target audience within the prompt entry, and submit. The AI will generate tailored ad copy to effectively reach different segments of your target audience on multiple platforms.

Eric Agyemang Duah

3. Developing a Social Media Content Calendar

Scenario

A social media manager needs to plan a month's worth of content for a new brand, ensuring a consistent posting schedule and diverse content types.

Prompt

"You are a social media strategist. Develop a one-month content calendar for [brand name, e.g., 'Aura Skincare'] targeting [target audience, e.g., women aged 25-45 interested in natural beauty]. Include daily post ideas, recommended platforms (Instagram, TikTok, Facebook), content formats (e.g., reels, stories, carousels), and key hashtags for each post."

How It Works

Using a tool like ChatGPT, Perplexity AI, or Gemini, first enter the prompt. Next, specify the brand name and target audience within the prompt entry, and submit. The AI will create a structured content plan, complete with themes, formats, and hashtags, to streamline your social media efforts.

4.   Product Image Editing for a Marketing Campaign

Scenario

A digital marketer needs to adapt a single product photograph into several different visual assets for a social media campaign. They need to change the background, maintain the product's look, and add new elements seamlessly.

Prompt

"You are a professional digital artist. Based on the attached product image, change the background to a sunny, outdoor cafe scene. Ensure the product's texture and lighting remain consistent with its original appearance."

How It Works

Using a tool like ChatGPT, Gemini (*Nano Banana*), or Canva AI, first, enter the prompt. Next, upload the image in a format like .jpeg or .png. Then, submit. The AI will provide the first-pass edit.

Follow-up Prompt

Once the first edit is complete, you can provide follow-up prompts to continue refining the image. The AI will remember the original image and all previous edits. For example, you can now enter: *"Now, add a second version of the same image. Change the cafe scene background to a vibrant city street at night and add a rainy effect."*

5. Creating a Product Explainer Video Script

Scenario
A marketing team needs an engaging script for a short product explainer video (60-90 seconds) to highlight key features and benefits for potential customers.

> ### Prompt
>
> *"You are a video content strategist. Draft a 60-90 second explainer video script for [insert product name, e.g., 'EcoCharge Portable Solar Charger']. Focus on key features, benefits, and a strong problem-solution narrative. Include visual cues for each scene, a compelling voice-over script, and a clear Call-to-Action."*

How It Works
Using a tool like ChatGPT, Gemini, or Canva AI, first enter the prompt, specifying the product name in the prompt entry. Next, submit. The AI will generate a detailed video script, complete with scene descriptions and voice-over text, ready for production.

6. Revitalizing an Underperforming Ad Campaign

Scenario

A marketing team's ad campaign for a new product isn't achieving expected engagement or conversions.

Prompt

"You are a digital marketing consultant. Analyze the provided ad copy or video script below for [e.g., Skincare Product Campaign]. Evaluate messaging, visuals, and targeting strategy. Provide specific recommendations to improve engagement and conversions, including revised copy, alternative scripts, creative ideas, and improved audience segmentation."

How It Works

Using a tool like ChatGPT or Gemini, first enter the prompt, specifying your product campaign within the prompt entry. Next, provide your ad text or video script below it and submit. The AI will critique and optimize messaging and creative elements for stronger ROI across campaign formats.

Medical Doctor

Essential Role of a Medical Doctor

Medical doctors diagnose, treat, and manage illnesses while guiding patients on preventive care. They interpret complex data, create treatment plans, and work with healthcare teams to improve patient outcomes.

Common Challenges Faced by Medical Doctors

Doctors face time constraints, extensive documentation, and the need to stay current with rapidly evolving medical knowledge. Interpreting lab results, imaging, and patient histories can overwhelm even experienced clinicians.

How AI Simplifies Medical Tasks

AI tools like ChatGPT, Gemini, and Perplexity AI help doctors by summarizing research, generating patient-friendly explanations, drafting documentation, and supporting differential diagnoses. These tools reduce administrative burdens, improve accuracy, and free up time for compassionate, patient-centered care, empowering doctors to deliver more efficient, informed, and personalized healthcare.

Eric Agyemang Duah

Crafting Effective Prompts for Medical Tasks

This section presents practical prompts showing doctors how to use AI tools like ChatGPT, Gemini, and Perplexity AI to improve efficiency in tasks like research summarization, patient communication, and clinical documentation. Each prompt includes a realistic scenario, a precise command, and an explanation of how AI-generated outputs enhance patient care and streamline medical workflows.

1. Summarizing Complex Research Papers

Scenario

A doctor needs to quickly understand a dense 30-page cardiology study before a patient consultation.

Prompt

"You are a medical researcher. Summarize the attached 30-page cardiology research paper in 500 words. Highlight study objectives, key findings, limitations, and clinical implications, maintaining medical accuracy and clarity."

How It Works

Using a tool like ChatGPT or Gemini, first upload the research paper in a format like .pdf or .docx. Next, enter the prompt and submit. The AI will condense the detailed study into a concise, clear summary to support evidence-based consultations.

2. Explaining Complex Lab Results to Patients

Scenario

A physician receives comprehensive lab panels with abnormal values and wants to explain them clearly to the patient.

Prompt

"You are an internal medicine physician. Translate the attached lab results, including abnormal liver enzymes and electrolytes, into clear, patient-friendly explanations. Describe what each abnormal value means, possible causes, and recommended next steps in language accessible to non-medical patients."

How It Works

Using a tool like ChatGPT, Perplexity AI, or Gemini, first upload the lab report in .pdf or image format. Next, enter the prompt and submit. The AI uses OCR to read the data and produces easy-to-understand explanations that facilitate patient communication.

3. Generating Differential Diagnosis Lists

Scenario

A doctor sees a patient with nonspecific symptoms like fatigue, weight loss, and night sweats, and needs a structured list of possible diagnoses.

Prompt

"You are an experienced diagnostician. Given symptoms of fatigue, unexplained weight loss, and night sweats, generate a prioritized differential diagnosis list. Include common and serious conditions, recommended initial tests, and brief rationales for each possibility."

How It Works

Using a tool like ChatGPT or Perplexity AI, first enter the prompt with the patient's symptoms. Next, submit. The AI will produce a structured, ranked list of possible diagnoses with suggested investigations, aiding diagnostic reasoning.

4. Creating Informed Consent Summaries

Scenario

A surgeon needs to provide a clear, understandable consent summary for a complex orthopedic procedure.

Prompt

You are a medical writer. Draft a patient-friendly informed consent summary for [e.g., total knee replacement surgery], explaining the procedure, risks, benefits, alternatives, and postoperative care in plain language suitable for patients with no medical background."

How It Works

Using a tool like ChatGPT, Gemini, or Perplexity AI, first enter the prompt, specifying the procedure details. Next, submit. The AI translates complex medical information into accessible consent material, facilitating ethical patient decision-making.

5. Managing Patients with Multiple Chronic Diseases

Scenario

A physician is treating a patient with hypertension, type 2 diabetes, and chronic kidney disease and needs a coordinated management plan.

Prompt

"You are a primary care physician. Draft an integrated care plan for a patient with hypertension, Type 2 diabetes, and stage 3 chronic kidney disease. Include medication adjustments, dietary and lifestyle guidance, and specialist referrals in patient-friendly language."

How It Works

Using a tool like ChatGPT, Perplexity AI, or Gemini, first enter the prompt with patient conditions. Next, submit. The AI synthesizes guidelines into a comprehensive, understandable management plan, promoting coordinated care.

6. Designing a Home Monitoring Protocol

Scenario

A doctor wants a plan for home monitoring of blood pressure, glucose, and weight for a heart failure patient.

Prompt

"You are a cardiologist. Develop a step-by-step home monitoring protocol for daily blood pressure, glucose, and weight tracking, including thresholds for concern and when to contact the clinic, presented in clear, patient-friendly language."

How It Works

Using a tool like ChatGPT or Perplexity AI, first enter the prompt with patient-specific details. Next, submit. The AI generates a tailored monitoring plan, empowering patients to detect early warning signs and engage with their healthcare team proactively.

Musician

Essential Role of a Musician

Musicians create, perform, arrange, and record music for diverse audiences and platforms. They compose original pieces, reinterpret existing works, and collaborate with other creatives to produce compelling musical content. Their contributions are essential in entertainment, education, cultural preservation, and emotional storytelling.

Common Challenges Faced by Musicians

Musicians often face challenges such as creative block, time-consuming composition processes, limited access to studio resources, and the complexity of music production tools. Additionally, independent artists may struggle with branding, marketing, and producing industry-level demos.

How AI Simplifies Musical Tasks

AI tools like Suno, ChatGPT, and Canva AI assist musicians with melody generation, lyric writing, arrangement ideas, and even producing fully synthesized audio. These tools help speed up music creation, overcome creative block, and enhance the quality of outputs—empowering musicians to focus on their artistic vision.

Crafting Effective Prompts for Musical Tasks

This section explores how musicians can strategically use AI tools like Suno, ChatGPT, Perplexity, Microsoft Copilot and Canva AI to streamline songwriting, arrangement, and creative production workflows. Each prompt includes a realistic scenario, a carefully constructed prompt, and a "How it works" explanation that outlines the tools' role in generating melodies, writing lyrics, or preparing professional-grade assets.

1. Generating Original Song Lyrics

Scenario

A singer-songwriter is experiencing creative block and needs emotionally resonant lyrics for a ballad about healing from heartbreak.

Prompt

You are a professional songwriter. Write emotionally expressive lyrics for a ballad titled "After the Storm," focusing on themes of heartbreak, inner strength, and emotional healing. Structure the lyrics with verses, a chorus, and a bridge.

How It Works

Using a tool like ChatGPT, Microsoft Copilot, or Perplexity AI, first enter the prompt. Next, submit. The AI will generate well-structured, emotionally resonant lyrics, providing a strong creative foundation for the songwriter to build upon.

2. Designing a Promotional Poster for a Music Release

Scenario

A musician is preparing to release a new jazz EP and wants a sleek promotional poster for social media.

Prompt

"Design a promotional poster for the release of a jazz EP titled 'Midnight Groove.' Include abstract saxophone art, dark blue and gold tones, the release date (July 21), and a QR code placeholder for streaming platforms."

How It Works

Using a tool like ChatGPT, Gemini, or Perplexity AI, first enter the prompt. Next, submit. The AI will suggest creative text and design ideas, which you can further refine and develop into a professional poster using graphic tools like Canva AI.

3. Genre-Blending Song Creation

Scenario

A songwriter wants to experiment by blending Afrobeats with Lo-fi elements for a niche streaming audience.

Prompt

"You are a songwriter creating a 90-second demo combining Afrobeats rhythms and percussion with Lo-fi textures and ambient melodies. The theme is 'sunrise on a quiet street in Accra.' Include vocals with subtle storytelling elements."

How It Works

Using a tool like Suno or Microsoft Copilot, first enter the prompt. Next, submit. The AI will generate a hybrid sound composition layering rhythmic and melodic elements, allowing experimentation with cross-genre production.

4. Refining a Gospel Song for Clarity and Impact

Scenario

A gospel musician has drafted a heartfelt worship song but feels the lyrics need refinement.

Prompt

"You are a gospel songwriter. Refine the provided worship song lyrics to improve lyrical flow, emotional resonance, and scriptural depth, while preserving the original voice and message. Ensure a consistent structure including verse, chorus, and bridge, with a reverent and uplifting tone."

How It Works

Using a tool like ChatGPT, Microsoft Copilot, or Perplexity AI, first enter the prompt. Next, paste your draft lyrics directly below it and submit. The AI will enhance structure, imagery, and word choice, delivering polished lyrics that maintain your spiritual intent.

5. Designing a Music Promotion Campaign

Scenario

An independent gospel artist is preparing to release a new single and wants a structured marketing plan to promote it across social media, email, and streaming platforms.

Prompt

"You are a digital music marketer. Develop a comprehensive 2-week promotional campaign for a gospel single release. Include daily content ideas, platform-specific strategies (Instagram, TikTok, YouTube Shorts), a pre-save link plan, fan engagement tactics, and email marketing tips. Tailor the campaign to an independent artist working with a modest budget."

How It Works

Using a tool like ChatGPT, Gemini, or Canva AI, first enter the prompt. Next, submit. The AI will create a detailed plan with platform-focused actions and engagement templates to drive organic growth within budget constraints.

6.   Preparing for Media Interviews on a New Music Release

Scenario

A rising artist is about to appear on radio and television to promote their debut single and needs to prepare for interviews.

Prompt

"You are a professional music publicist coaching a new artist for their first radio and TV interviews about their debut single. Develop a 2-minute personal narrative, key talking points, anticipated questions with sample responses, and tips for confident delivery, tone, posture, and adapting to different interview formats."

How It Works

Using a tool like ChatGPT or Gemini, first enter the prompt. Next, submit. The AI will generate a complete media coaching brief to help the artist effectively communicate their story and engage audiences professionally.

Pharmacist

Essential Role of a Pharmacist

Pharmacists ensure the safe and effective use of medications by dispensing prescriptions, advising on dosage, identifying drug interactions, and counseling patients. They serve as a critical bridge between prescribers and patients in the healthcare system.

Common Challenges Faced by Pharmacists

Pharmacists often face time constraints, complex drug regimens, frequent updates in pharmacology, and challenges in patient adherence. Managing high prescription volumes while ensuring accuracy and patient understanding adds to their workload.

How AI Simplifies Pharmacy Tasks

AI tools like ChatGPT, Gemini, and Perplexity AI help pharmacists streamline patient counseling, check drug interactions, summarize treatment protocols, and create educational materials. This enhances clinical accuracy, improves patient communication, and supports informed, efficient decision-making in both retail and clinical settings.

Crafting Effective Prompts for Pharmacy Tasks

This section presents practical AI prompts tailored for pharmacists, helping them optimize core responsibilities like medication counseling, interaction checking, and clinical communication. Using large language models (LLMs) such as ChatGPT, Gemini, and Perplexity AI, pharmacists can enhance efficiency, accuracy, and patient safety in daily workflows. Each prompt features a realistic scenario, a strategically designed prompt, and a brief explanation of how the AI's response supports pharmaceutical decision-making.

1. Counseling on New Medication Use

Scenario

A pharmacist needs to explain metformin to a newly diagnosed type 2 diabetes patient.

> ### Prompt
>
> *You are a clinical pharmacist. Explain to a newly diagnosed type 2 diabetes patient how metformin works, how to take it safely, and possible side effects. Use clear, non-technical language suitable for patient understanding.*

How It Works

Using a tool like ChatGPT, Perplexity AI, or Gemini, first enter the prompt. Next, submit. The AI will generate a concise, patient-friendly explanation that enhances understanding and supports safe medication use.

Eric Agyemang Duah

2. Detecting Potential Drug Interactions

Scenario

A pharmacist is reviewing a patient's medication list and wants to check for possible interactions between prescribed drugs and recent over-the-counter supplements.

> ### *Prompt*
>
> *"You are a clinical pharmacist. Review a patient's list of prescribed medications and recent over-the-counter supplements provided below. Identify potential drug-drug or drug-supplement interactions and explain their clinical significance in concise terms."*

How It Works

Using a tool like ChatGPT or Gemini, first enter the prompt. Next, paste the complete list of medications and supplements as text directly below it and submit. The AI will analyze interaction risks and provide clinical explanations to support therapy adjustments or patient counseling.

3. Generating Patient-Friendly Drug Guides

Scenario

A pharmacist needs to provide a simplified drug information leaflet to a patient starting a new prescription.

Prompt

"You are a drug information pharmacist. Generate a patient-friendly drug guide for [insert drug name], including its purpose, dosage instructions, common side effects, storage advice, and safety tips. Use simple language appropriate for a non-medical audience."

How It Works

Using a tool like ChatGPT, Perplexity AI, or Gemini, first enter the prompt with the medication name. Next, submit. The AI will deliver an easy-to-understand, pharmacist-grade guide suitable for patients with limited medical knowledge.

4. Supporting Geriatric Polypharmacy Management

Scenario

A pharmacist is managing a senior patient with multiple chronic conditions taking over ten medications. They must assess for safety and adherence.

Prompt

"You are a professional pharmacist. Review the following geriatric patient's medication list. Identify polypharmacy concerns such as therapeutic duplication, inappropriate dosing, high-risk interactions, or administration challenges. Recommend a simplified regimen aligned with geriatric pharmacotherapy best practices."

How It Works

Using a tool like ChatGPT or Perplexity AI, first enter the prompt. Next, paste the complete medication list as text directly below it and submit. The AI will identify risks and suggest optimization strategies for safer, more manageable therapy.

5. Oncology Medication Verification and Side Effect Profiling

Scenario

A hospital pharmacist must verify a complex chemotherapy order for a breast cancer patient. They also need to counsel the patient about expected side effects.

Prompt

"You are an oncology pharmacist. Review the following chemotherapy regimen for a breast cancer patient. Verify dosing, check for drug interactions, and summarize expected side effects, monitoring requirements, and key counseling points."

How It Works

Using a tool like ChatGPT or Gemini, first enter the prompt. Next, upload or paste the chemotherapy plan as PDF or text with relevant lab results, and submit. The AI will cross-check dosing standards, highlight contraindications, and generate an accessible patient education summary.

6. Remote Counseling via Telepharmacy

Scenario

A rural pharmacist providing telepharmacy services needs to offer a concise medication counseling session for a newly discharged heart failure patient.

> ### *Prompt*
>
> *"You are a clinical pharmacist providing telepharmacy services. Prepare a simplified, patient-friendly explanation of carvedilol, lisinopril, and furosemide for a newly discharged heart failure patient, covering drug purpose, administration timing, side effects, and warning signs."*

How It Works

Using a tool like ChatGPT or perplexity AI, first enter the prompt. Next, submit. The AI will create a clear, comprehensive guide designed for virtual counseling, supporting effective patient understanding without in-person contact.

Soccer Coach

Essential Role of a Soccer Coach

A soccer coach guides individual players and entire teams toward peak performance through tactical training, physical conditioning, and motivational leadership. Coaches develop game strategies, assess opponents, and make real-time decisions during matches to optimize outcomes.

Common Challenges Faced by Soccer Coaches

Soccer coaches often struggle with creating personalized training regimens, analyzing opponent strategies, balancing team dynamics, and scouting emerging talent. Time constraints and limited access to advanced analytics also hinder strategic planning.

How AI Simplifies Soccer Coaching Tasks

AI tools such as ChatGPT, Gemini, and Perplexity AI streamline scouting reports, generate game plans, analyze match statistics, and suggest training drills tailored to player needs. These platforms can evaluate player performance trends and simulate opponent tactics, enabling coaches to make data-informed decisions that enhance team cohesion and competitive edge.

Crafting Effective Prompts for Soccer Coaching Tasks

This section presents targeted prompts designed to assist soccer coaches in optimizing tactical planning, player development, and match preparation using tools like ChatGPT, Gemini, and Perplexity AI. Each prompt includes a real-world coaching scenario, a precision-crafted prompt, and a clear explanation of how the AI processes user input to generate actionable insights that align with team and performance objectives.

1. Designing a Weekly Training Schedule

Scenario

A soccer coach wants to structure a balanced weekly training schedule for a U-17 team focused on fitness, technical skills, and match tactics.

Prompt

You are a youth soccer coach. Create a detailed 5-day training schedule for a U-17 team focusing on fitness, ball control, positional drills, and tactical scrimmages. Ensure the plan balances physical conditioning and technical skills, tailored to the age and skill level of the players.

How It Works

Using a tool like ChatGPT, Perplexity AI, or Gemini, first enter the prompt. Next, submit. The AI will generate a day-by-day training plan structured to optimize fitness, technical development, and tactical understanding.

2. Tactical Breakdown from Match Footage

Scenario

A soccer coach wants to evaluate their team's defensive structure during a recent match to identify weaknesses in transition after losing possession.

Prompt

Act as a professional football tactical analyst. Analyze the attached 10-minute match video focusing on defensive transitions during the first half. Our team wears blue jerseys and started on the left side of the pitch. Evaluate defensive shape, player spacing, and recovery after turnovers, then recommend tactical improvements.

How It Works

Using a tool like ChatGPT Plus/Pro, or Gemini Pro, first enter the prompt. Next, upload the match footage in a format like .mp4. Then, submit. The AI provides a professional tactical report highlighting defensive strengths, weaknesses, and suggested strategies.

3. Pre-Match Strategy Development

Scenario

A soccer coach is preparing for an upcoming match against a team known for high pressing and rapid wing play.

Prompt

"Act as a seasoned football strategist. Draft a pre-match tactical plan to counter an opponent known for high pressing and rapid wing play. Our team excels at midfield control and long-ball transitions. Suggest formations, in-possession and out-of-possession tactics, and key player roles to exploit weaknesses in the opponent's press."

How It Works

Using a tool like ChatGPT, Perplexity AI, or Gemini, first enter the prompt. Next, submit. The AI will produce a comprehensive game plan tailored to your team's strengths and the opposition's playing style.

Eric Agyemang Duah

4. Post-Match Performance Analysis

Scenario

A soccer coach wants to critically analyze their team's performance based on key tactical objectives to guide the next week's training focus.

Prompt

"You are a professional football performance analyst. Based on the attached match video, evaluate our team's performance on possession control, transition speed, and defensive organization. Highlight strengths, weaknesses, and recommend three key training focus areas. Our team wears red and white jerseys and started on the right side of the pitch."

How It Works

Using a tool like ChatGPT Plus/Pro, or Gemini Pro, first enter the prompt. Next, upload the video in a format like .mp4. Then, submit. The AI generates a concise evaluation report with actionable insights to guide future training sessions.

5. Designing a Position-Specific Training Plan

Scenario

A soccer coach wants to create a focused training routine for central midfielders to improve spatial awareness, passing under pressure, and defensive positioning.

Prompt

"You are a UEFA-certified football coach. Design a detailed 5-day training plan specifically for central midfielders to improve spatial awareness, quick passing under pressure, and defensive positioning against high-pressing teams. Include drill names, session duration, and objectives."

How It Works

Using a tool like ChatGPT or Perplexity AI, first enter the prompt. Next, submit. The AI will create a targeted training schedule to improve tactical and technical proficiency at a critical position.

6. Designing Position-Specific Drills

Scenario

A soccer coach is preparing a midweek training session focused on improving winger performance.

Prompt

"You are an elite football development coach. Design a 90-minute winger-focused training session that improves acceleration, crossing accuracy under pressure, and decision-making in the final third. Include drill names, duration, required equipment, and coaching points."

How It Works

Using a tool like ChatGPT or Perplexity AI, first enter the prompt. Next, submit. The AI will generate a structured session plan with warm-ups, technical drills, cooldowns, and coaching tips designed to maximize winger performance.

Software Engineer

Essential Role of a Software Engineer

Software engineers design, develop, test, and maintain software systems that power applications, websites, embedded systems, and enterprise tools. They translate technical specifications into functional code, solve complex problems, optimize performance, and ensure scalability and security. Their work forms the digital infrastructure for businesses, governments, and global platforms.

Common Challenges Faced by Software Engineers

Software engineers often face tight deadlines, debugging bottlenecks, integration complexities, and ambiguous feature requests. Managing large codebases, ensuring cross-platform compatibility, and writing efficient, maintainable code require significant time and focus.

How AI Simplifies Software Engineering Tasks

AI tools like ChatGPT, Canva AI, Gemini, Microsoft Copilot, and Perplexity AI assist software engineers by generating boilerplate code, debugging, suggesting architecture patterns, optimizing queries, translating pseudocode into code, and reviewing logic. These tools accelerate development workflows, reduce cognitive load, and improve productivity across the software lifecycle.

Crafting Effective Prompts for Software Engineering Tasks

This section presents strategic prompts tailored for software engineers seeking to accelerate development, troubleshoot issues, and streamline project workflows using tools like ChatGPT, Gemini, Canva AI, and Microsoft Copilot. Whether you are prototyping, optimizing algorithms, documenting APIs, or reviewing code, each prompt features a realistic scenario, an optimized prompt, and a clearly explained outcome to demonstrate how AI can enhance modern software engineering tasks with efficiency and precision.

1. Debugging an Authentication Error

Scenario

A software engineer encounters a persistent login failure in a web app's authentication flow.

> ### *Prompt*
>
> *"You are a senior software engineer. Analyze this authentication error log and identify the root cause. Suggest a fix and best practices to prevent similar issues."*

How It Works

Using a tool like ChatGPT or Gemini, first enter the prompt. Next, paste the error log as plain text (.txt)   directly below it, and submit. The AI will diagnose the issue and propose actionable solutions.

2. Refactoring Legacy Code for Performance

Scenario

A software engineer is tasked with optimizing a legacy codebase that is slowing down application performance.

Prompt

"You are a software engineer. Refactor the legacy code provided below to improve performance, readability, and maintainability. Include inline comments to explain your changes and suggest further architectural improvements if applicable."

How It Works

Using a tool like ChatGPT, Microsoft Copilot, or Gemini, first enter the prompt. Next, paste the legacy code snippet from a text-based file (.txt, .py, .js) directly below it, and submit. The AI will analyze inefficiencies, refactor the code for improved readability, performance, and maintainability, and include inline comments explaining the changes.

3. Generating API Documentation

Scenario

A software engineer needs to quickly generate clear documentation for a new RESTful API.

Prompt

"You are a software engineer. Generate complete and developer-friendly API documentation for the following endpoints, including request/response examples, parameters, error codes, and authentication requirements."

How It Works

Using a tool like ChatGPT, Perplexity AI, or Gemini, first enter the prompt. Next, paste the relevant API code or route definitions from a text-based file (.txt, .js, .py) directly below it, and submit. The AI will generate complete, developer-friendly API documentation suitable for developer portals or onboarding.

4. Debugging Complex Code Logic

Scenario

A software engineer encounters a persistent logical error in a backend service handling dynamic pricing algorithms.

Prompt

"You are a senior backend developer. Analyze the following Python function for logic errors affecting dynamic price calculation and suggest precise fixes with a brief explanation."

How It Works

Using a tool like ChatGPT, Microsoft Copilot, or Gemini, first enter the prompt. Next, paste the problematic code from a text-based file (.txt, .py) directly below it, and submit. The AI will analyze the logic, identify edge cases or faulty conditions, and recommend corrected code with clear inline commentary.

5. Reviewing Algorithm Efficiency

Scenario

A software engineer is optimizing a Python algorithm that performs data filtering on large datasets. They want an analysis of its time and space complexity.

> ### *Prompt*
>
> *"You are a senior software engineer. Review the following Python algorithm for time and space complexity. Identify any inefficiencies and propose optimization strategies without changing the algorithm's core logic."*

How It Works

Using a tool like ChatGPT or Gemini, first enter the prompt. Next, paste the full Python algorithm from a Python file (.py) directly below it, and submit. The AI will evaluate the algorithm's time and space complexity, identify inefficiencies, and propose optimization strategies that preserve the core logic.

6. Designing RESTful API Endpoints

Scenario
A backend software engineer is tasked with developing a RESTful API for a bookstore management system.

> ### *Prompt*
>
> *"You are a backend engineer. Design RESTful API endpoints for a bookstore system that allows listing all books, retrieving book details by ID, updating inventory levels, and managing customer orders. Ensure proper use of HTTP methods and endpoint structure."*

How It Works
Using a tool like ChatGPT, Canva AI, or Gemini, first enter the prompt. Next, submit. The AI will create a set of well-structured RESTful API endpoints, recommending URI paths, HTTP methods (GET, POST, PUT, DELETE), and concise descriptions of functionality.

Teacher

Essential Role of a Teacher

Teachers design and deliver curriculum-aligned instruction, assess learner progress, and adapt pedagogy to accommodate varying abilities and learning styles. They cultivate intellectual curiosity, critical thinking, and social development, serving as foundational figures in students' academic and personal growth.

Common Challenges Faced by Teachers

Teachers face time constraints, large class sizes, administrative burdens, and the need to differentiate instruction for diverse learners. Maintaining engagement, designing inclusive content, managing assessments, and staying current with evolving standards further compound their workload.

How AI Simplifies Teaching Tasks

AI platforms such as ChatGPT, Perplexity AI, Gemini, and Microsoft Copilot support teachers by generating lesson plans, quizzes, grading rubrics, and personalized activities. These tools help reduce repetitive tasks, accelerate content creation, and enhance instructional design—enabling teachers to focus more on interactive and student-centered learning experiences.

Crafting Effective Prompts for Teaching Tasks

This section presents structured prompts tailored to core teaching responsibilities. Each prompt addresses real classroom tasks—lesson planning, assessment design, feedback, and differentiated instruction—optimized for platforms like ChatGPT, Gemini, Perplexity AI, and Microsoft Copilot to support pedagogical effectiveness.

1. Hands-On Math Lesson Planning

Scenario

An elementary school teacher needs to design a dynamic and interactive math lesson on a challenging concept like fractions, using engaging methods to ensure young students grasp the topic.

Prompt

"You are an elementary math teacher in an urban school. Design a hands-on math lesson on fractions for a 3rd-grade class, using visual aids and real-world examples to make the concepts accessible and fun. The lesson should include interactive games, manipulatives, and problem-solving exercises that reinforce the understanding of fractions and their applications."

How It Works

Using a tool like ChatGPT, Microsoft Copilot, or Gemini, first, enter the prompt exactly as it is written. Then, submit. The AI will generate a structured lesson plan complete with activity ideas and real-world examples to make fractions easier to teach and learn.

2. Interactive Activities for Special Education

Scenario

A special education teacher needs a collection of interactive, accessible activities to reinforce core language arts skills for students with learning disabilities.

> ### *Prompt*
>
> *"Assume you are a special education teacher working with a group of 4th-grade students with learning disabilities. Create a set of 10 interactive activities that can be used during a language arts lesson to reinforce vocabulary, reading comprehension, and writing skills in an engaging and accessible manner."*

How It Works

Using a tool like ChatGPT or Gemini, first, enter the prompt exactly as it is written. Then, submit. The AI will provide a list of tailored activities that can be immediately implemented in the classroom to support the students' learning needs.

3. Creating Differentiated Practice Exercises

Scenario

A teacher needs differentiated reading tasks for Grade 5 students at varying ability levels.

Prompt

"You are a professional 5th grade English teacher in an urban public school. Using the learning objective provided below, create three differentiated English practice activities—one each for advanced, intermediate, and emerging readers. For each activity, include a short nonfiction passage, clear instructions, response tasks, and the correct answers."

How It Works

Using a tool like ChatGPT or Perplexity AI, first enter the prompt. Next, paste the learning objective from a text-based file (.txt, .docx) directly below it, then submit. The AI will generate leveled practice activities, each with corresponding nonfiction passages, instructions, and answer keys.

4. Generating Formative Quiz Questions

Scenario

A teacher wants to assess students' understanding of a Grade 8 science topic—photosynthesis—through a quick formative quiz.

Prompt

"You are a professional science teacher. Based on the topic of photosynthesis and the Grade 8 science standard provided below, generate a 10-question formative quiz. Include a mix of multiple-choice, short-answer, and true/false items. Provide the correct answers after each question."

How It Works

Using a tool like ChatGPT or Perplexity AI, first enter the prompt. Next, paste the relevant standard from a text-based file (.txt, .docx) directly below it, then submit. The AI will create a 10-question formative quiz aligned with the standard, featuring a mix of question types and an answer key.

Eric Agyemang Duah

5. Writing Personalized Student Feedback

Scenario

A teacher has reviewed a set of student essays and wants to generate constructive, individualized feedback.

Prompt

"You are a professional teacher. Based on the student's essay excerpt and rubric score provided below, write personalized feedback highlighting one strength, one area for improvement, and a final encouraging remark. Keep the tone constructive and student-friendly."

How It Works

Using a tool like ChatGPT, Gemini, or Microsoft Copilot, first, use a scanning app like Google Lens on your phone to convert the hardcopy essay into a text-based file (.txt, .docx). Next, enter the prompt, paste the essay excerpt and rubric scores directly below it, and submit. The AI will generate personalized, constructive feedback with a positive, student-friendly tone

6. Designing a Conceptual Quiz on Newton's Laws

Scenario

A physics teacher is introducing Newton's Laws and needs a short quiz to check students' conceptual understanding.

> ### *Prompt*
>
> *"You are a professional physics teacher. Create a 10-question conceptual quiz on Newton's three laws of motion for high school students. Use a mix of multiple-choice and short-answer questions. Provide an answer key."*

How It Works

Using a tool like ChatGPT or Perplexity AI, first enter the prompt. Next, submit. The AI will generate a 10-question conceptual quiz on Newton's three laws of motion for high school students, with a mix of multiple-choice and short-answer formats, and correct answers.

Technical Writer

Essential Role of a Technical Writer

Technical writers transform complex technical information into clear, accessible documentation. They create manuals, user guides, API references, and instructional content that support end users, developers, and stakeholders. Their writing ensures that products and systems can be understood, used, and maintained efficiently.

Common Challenges Faced by Technical Writers

Technical writers often face challenges such as incomplete technical input, tight deadlines, rapidly changing specifications, and the need to balance clarity with technical accuracy. Maintaining consistency across documentation formats and ensuring content aligns with both user needs and product updates can be demanding.

How AI Simplifies Technical Writing Tasks

AI tools like ChatGPT, Perplexity, Microsoft Copilot, and Gemini assist technical writers by generating structured drafts, rewriting complex content for clarity, maintaining style consistency, summarizing technical notes, and suggesting formatting improvements. These tools accelerate documentation workflows, reduce editing time, and support scalable, user-friendly content production.

Eric Agyemang Duah

Crafting Effective Prompts for Technical Writing Tasks

This section presents professionally aligned prompts tailored to the key responsibilities of technical writers. Each prompt reflects real-world documentation tasks and is optimized for AI tools like ChatGPT, Perplexity AI, Gemini, or Microsoft Copilot. They help writers produce accurate, accessible, and user-centered content efficiently across technical and product documentation workflows.

1. Drafting a User Guide Section

Scenario

A technical writer needs to draft a user guide section for a new software feature that is part of a larger product launch.

> ### *Prompt*
>
> *"You are a technical writer. Based on the feature description provided below, draft a clear, user-friendly guide section. Include step-by-step instructions, use cases, and expected outputs."*

How It Works

Using a tool like ChatGPT, Perplexity AI, or Gemini, first enter the prompt. Next, paste the feature description from a text-based file (.txt, .docx) directly below it and submit. The AI will generate a well-structured, task-oriented section ready for documentation.

2. Converting Technical Notes into Formal Documentation

Scenario

A technical writer receives fragmented engineering notes from a developer describing a new API function. The writer must convert these into formal, standardized documentation suitable for publication.

> ### Prompt
>
> *"You are a technical writer. Convert the technical notes provided below into formal API documentation. Include function purpose, parameters, return types, usage examples, and formatting aligned with documentation standards."*

How It Works

Using a tool like ChatGPT, Gemini, or Microsoft Copilot, first enter the prompt. Next, paste the raw technical notes and specifications from a text-based file (.txt, .docx) directly below it and submit. The AI will transform the notes into formal, standardized API documentation.

Eric Agyemang Duah

3. Writing Patient Information Leaflets for a Pharmaceutical Product

Scenario

A technical writer is assigned to draft a patient information leaflet for an over-the-counter medication, ensuring clarity, regulatory compliance, and accessibility for non-expert readers.

> ### Prompt
>
> *"You are a technical writer. Based on the product information provided, write a patient information leaflet (PIL) for a pharmaceutical product. Include sections on usage, dosage, precautions, side effects, and storage. Ensure the tone is accessible to the general public."*

How It Works

Using a tool like ChatGPT or Gemini, first enter the prompt. Next, paste the product data sheet or formulation details from a text-based file (.txt, .pdf) directly below it and submit. The AI will produce a clear, easy-to-understand patient information leaflet that is compliant with health literacy and regulatory requirements.

4. Drafting Operating Instructions for a Medical Device

Scenario

A technical writer wants to produce clear operating instructions for a portable ECG monitoring device used by healthcare professionals in outpatient settings.

> ### Prompt
>
> *"You are a technical writer. Using the device specifications provided below, draft operating instructions for a portable ECG machine. Include setup steps, usage procedures, safety notes, and indications for troubleshooting."*

How It Works

Using a tool like ChatGPT, Perplexity AI, or Gemini, first enter the prompt. Next, paste the device specifications from a text-based file (.txt, .docx) directly below it and submit. The AI will create professional, clinical-grade operating instructions covering setup, usage, safety precautions, and troubleshooting guidance.

5. Creating a Troubleshooting Guide for a Vehicle Infotainment System

Scenario

A technical writer is documenting a troubleshooting section for a car's infotainment system manual, aimed at non-technical vehicle owners.

> ### *Prompt*
>
> *"You are a technical writer. Based on the issues listed below, write a troubleshooting section for a vehicle infotainment system. Include problem symptoms, likely causes, and clear user-level solutions."*

How It Works

Using a tool like ChatGPT, Perplexity AI, or Gemini, first enter the prompt. Next, paste a list of common issues and system notes from a text-based file (.txt, .docx) directly below it and submit. The AI will generate a structured troubleshooting section in user-friendly language.

Eric Agyemang Duah

6. Writing Assembly Instructions for a Home Appliance

Scenario

A technical writer is tasked with creating step-by-step assembly instructions for a consumer appliance, such as an air purifier or standing fan.

> ### Prompt
>
> *"You are a technical writer. Using the mechanical specifications and part list provided below, write step-by-step assembly instructions for this home appliance. Use clear, numbered steps and reference labeled parts."*

How It Works

Using a tool like ChatGPT or Gemini, first enter the prompt. Next, paste the part list and manufacturer notes from a text-based file (.txt, .docx) directly below it and submit. The AI will produce clear, stepwise assembly instructions.

Conclusion

This chapter has demonstrated how large language models can be effectively embedded within the operational realities of professional practice. Through strategically designed, domain-specific prompt packs, we have shown that prompt engineering is not merely a technical utility, but a practical method for improving clarity, precision, and efficiency across diverse sectors.

Each scenario exemplifies how professionals can frame inquiries, structure information, and co-create intelligent outputs with AI systems. While the prompts presented offer structured guidance, their deeper purpose is to cultivate adaptive thinking—empowering users to translate general prompting techniques (e.g., role-playing, chain-of-thought, zero-shot, few-shot) into meaningful, contextualized applications.

As professionals engage with AI across increasingly complex tasks, the ability to design thoughtful, goal-oriented prompts will prove indispensable. Prompting thus emerges not only as a skill of the future, but as a mental discipline fostering thoughtful and responsible professional practice in the present.

Acknowledgment

This book, **Perfect Prompting,** owes its existence and specialized insights to numerous individuals and institutions.

My deepest gratitude goes to the Microsoft and LinkedIn Learning instructors whose expert guidance on generative AI, prompt engineering, and the evolution of intelligent search profoundly shaped my work. The privilege of previewing their invaluable content was instrumental; their collective thought leadership inspired the central question that opens this book: *"How can we work intelligently with AI?"*

Special thanks are extended to several key thought leaders for their foundational contributions:

- Pinar Seyhan Demirdag (Generative AI Expert and AI Director at Cuebric) for her foundational insights into generative AI.

- Ronnie Sheer for his exceptionally clear teaching on prompt engineering principles.

- Ashley Kennedy (Managing Staff Instructor at LinkedIn Learning), Noelle Silver (Award-Winning Technologist and Microsoft MVP in AI), and Brandie Nonnecke (Founding Director, CITRIS Policy Lab, UC Berkeley), whose collective work on *The Evolution of Thoughtful Online Search* offered critical context on how reasoning engines are redefining digital inquiry.

Finally, I wish to express my sincere appreciation to the developers and research teams behind the AI tools that supported this book's creation.

ChatGPT and Perplexity were invaluable resources for preliminary research and early draft refinement, while Gemini provided essential professional editing and clarity support. These tools not only contributed significantly to the precision of the content but also exemplify the evolving potential of collaborative human–AI creativity.

References

AI fundamentals: What is Artificial Intelligence

1. Russell, S., & Norvig, P. (2020). *Artificial Intelligence: A Modern Approach* (4th ed.). Pearson.
2. Goodfellow, I., Bengio, Y., & Courville, A. (2016). *Deep Learning*. MIT Press.
3. Esteva, A., Kuprel, B., Novoa, R. A., Ko, J., Swetter, S. M., Blau, H. M., & Thrun, S. (2017). *Dermatologist-level classification of skin cancer with deep neural networks*. Nature, 542(7639), 115–118.
4. Mitchell, M. (2019). *Artificial Intelligence: A Guide for Thinking Humans*. Farrar, Straus and Giroux.
5. Nilsson, N. J. (2010). *The Quest for Artificial Intelligence: A History of Ideas and Achievements*. Cambridge University Press.

Key elements of AI

1. Mitchell, T. M. (1997). *Machine Learning*. McGraw-Hill.
2. Jurafsky, D., & Martin, J. H. (2023). *Speech and Language Processing* (3rd ed.). Pearson.
3. Szeliski, R. (2022). *Computer Vision: Algorithms and Applications* (2nd ed.). Springer.
4. Craig, J. J. (2005). *Introduction to Robotics: Mechanics and Control* (3rd ed.). Pearson.

Types of AI

1. .Nilsson, N. J. (2010). *The Quest for Artificial Intelligence: A History of Ideas and Achievements*. Cambridge University Press.
2. Russell, S. (2020). *Human Compatible: Artificial Intelligence and the Problem of Control*. Penguin Press.
3. Bostrom, N. (2014). *Superintelligence: Paths, Dangers, Strategies*. Oxford University Press.
4. Goertzel, B. & Pennachin, C. (2007). *Artificial General Intelligence*. Springer.
5. OpenAI. "GPT-4 Technical Report." OpenAI, 2023.
6. Tegmark, M. (2017). *Life 3.0: Being Human in the Age of Artificial Intelligence*. Knopf.

7. Yudkowsky, E. (2008). *Artificial Intelligence as a Positive and Negative Factor in Global Risk*. In Bostrom & Ćirković (Eds.), *Global Catastrophic Risks*. Oxford University Press.

Narrow AI

1. OpenAI. *"GPT-4 Technical Report."* OpenAI Research, 2023.
2. Anthropic. *"Claude 2: A Safer LLM."* Anthropic Research Blog, 2023.
3. Ricci, F., Rokach, L., & Shapira, B. (2015). *Recommender Systems Handbook*. Springer.
4. Garvie, C., Bedoya, A., & Frankle, J. (2016). *The Perpetual Line-Up: Unregulated Police Face Recognition in America*. Georgetown Law, Center on Privacy & Technology.
5. Jumper, J. et al. (2021). *"Highly accurate protein structure prediction with AlphaFold."* Nature, 596(7873), 583–589.
6. Aidoc. *"AI Radiology Solutions."* Accessed 2025. https://www.aidoc.com
7. Mastercard. *"Decision Intelligence for Fraud Prevention."* Mastercard Insights, 2022.
8. Hoy, M. B. (2018). *"Alexa, Siri, Cortana, and More: An Introduction to Voice Assistants."* Medical Reference Services Quarterly, 37(1), 81–88.

Transforming Industries with AI

1. McKinsey Global Institute. (2018). *AI Adoption Advances, but Foundational Barriers Remain*.
2. Esteva, A., et al. (2017). *Dermatologist-level classification of skin cancer with deep neural networks*. Nature, 542(7639), 115–118.
3. Arner, D. W., Barberis, J., & Buckley, R. P. (2016). *The evolution of Fintech: A new post-crisis paradigm*. Georgetown Journal of International Law, 47, 1271–1319.
4. Holmes, W., Bialik, M., & Fadel, C. (2019). *Artificial Intelligence in Education: Promises and Implications for Teaching and Learning*. Center for Curriculum Redesign.
5. Lee, J., et al. (2015). *Predictive Manufacturing System—Trends of Next-Generation Production Systems*. Procedia CIRP, 33, 233–238.
6. Grewal, D., et al. (2020). *The future of retailing*. Journal of Retailing, 96(1), 69–89.
7. Litman, T. (2020). *Autonomous vehicle implementation predictions*. Victoria Transport Policy Institute.
8. Seaver, N. (2019). *Captivating algorithms: Recommender systems as traps*. Journal of Material Culture, 24(4), 421–436.

Ethical and Societal Challenges in AI

1. Buolamwini, J., & Gebru, T. (2018). *Gender shades: Intersectional accuracy disparities in commercial gender classification*. Proceedings of Machine Learning Research, 81, 1–15.
2. Zuboff, S. (2019). *The Age of Surveillance Capitalism*. PublicAffairs.
3. Rudin, C. (2019). *Stop explaining black box machine learning models for high-stakes decisions and use interpretable models instead*. Nature Machine Intelligence, 1(5), 206–215.

4. Brynjolfsson, E., & McAfee, A. (2014). *The Second Machine Age*. W. W. Norton & Company.

5. Calo, R. (2015). Robotics and the lessons of cyberlaw. *California Law Review, 103(3),* 513–563.

6. Taylor, L., Floridi, L., & Van der Sloot, B. (Eds.). (2017). *Group Privacy: New Challenges of Data Technologies*. Springer.

7. European Commission. (2021). *Proposal for a Regulation Laying Down Harmonised Rules on Artificial Intelligence (Artificial Intelligence Act)*. Brussels.

8. Bostrom, N. (2014). *Superintelligence: Paths, Dangers, Strategies*. Oxford University Press

What is Prompt Engineering

1. Reynolds, L., & McDonell, K. (2021). Prompt Programming for Large Language Models: Beyond the Few-Shot Paradigm. *arXiv preprint arXiv:2102.07350*.

2. Brown, T. B., et al. (2020). Language models are few-shot learners. *Advances in Neural Information Processing Systems, 33,* 1877–1901.

3. Surden, H. (2014). Machine Learning and Law. *Washington Law Review, 89(1),* 87–115.

4. Holmes, W., Bialik, M., & Fadel, C. (2019). *Artificial Intelligence in Education: Promises and Implications for Teaching and Learning*. Center for Curriculum Redesign.

5. Esteva, A., et al. (2019). A guide to deep learning in healthcare. *Nature Medicine, 25(1),* 24–29.

6. Chui, M., et al. (2018). Notes from the AI frontier: Applications and value of deep learning. *McKinsey Global Institute Discussion Paper*.

7. Pearce, H., et al. (2023). Asleep at the Keyboard? Assessing the Security of GitHub Copilot's Code Contributions. *IEEE Symposium on Security and Privacy*.

8. Weidinger, L., et al. (2022). Ethical and social risks of harm from language models. *Proceedings of the 2022 ACM Conference on Fairness, Accountability, and Transparency*.

Advanced Prompting Techniques

1. Brown, T. B., et al. (2020). Language models are few-shot learners. *Advances in Neural Information Processing Systems, 33,* 1877–1901.

2. Kojima, T., et al. (2022). Large Language Models are Zero-Shot Reasoners. *arXiv preprint arXiv:2205.11916*.

3. Wei, J., et al. (2022). Chain-of-thought prompting elicits reasoning in large language models. *arXiv preprint arXiv:2201.11903*.

4. OpenAI. (2023). GPT-4 Technical Report. Retrieved from *https://openai.com/research/gpt-4*

5. Reimers, N., & Gurevych, I. (2020). Making Monolingual Sentence Embeddings Multilingual using Knowledge Distillation. *Proceedings of the 2020 Conference on Empirical Methods in Natural Language Processing (EMNLP)*.

AI Tools and Their Effective Use Cases

Openai (2025) https://openai.com/research/gpt-4

Google DeepMind (2025). https://deepmind.google/technologies/gemini

Perplexity AI (2025). https://www.perplexity.ai

Microsoft (2025). https://www.microsoft.com/copilot

Suno (2025). https://www.suno.com

Midjourney (2025). https://www.midjourney.com

Canva (2025). Magic Studio & Visual Suite 2.0 Features (canva.com)

Leonardo AI (2025). Phoenix & Creative Suite leonardo.ai (fahimai.com, youtube.com)

Cuebric & Disguise partnership (2023–2025)(disguise.one). (livedesignonline.com)

InVideo (2025). (help.invideo.io).

Limitations of AI

1. *Bender, E. M., Gebru, T., McMillan-Major, A., & Shmitchell, S. (2021). On the Dangers of Stochastic*

2. *Parrots: Can Language Models Be Too Big? Proceedings of the 2021 ACM Conference on Fairness, Accountability, and Transparency.*

3. *OpenAI (2024). GPT-4 Technical Report. https://openai.com/research/gpt-4*

4. *Anthropic (2024). Claude 3 System Card. https://www.anthropic.com/index/claude-3*

5. *Google DeepMind (2024). Gemini Technical Overview. https://deepmind.google/technologies/gemini*

6. *European Commission (2024). AI Act: Regulation on Artificial Intelligence. https://artificialintelligenceact.eu*

7. *EPI (2023). AI Hallucinations and Misinformation Risks. Ethics and Policy Initiative.*

About the Author

Eric Agyemang Duah is a recognized Generative AI specialist, author, and consultant focused on the practical application of AI-powered solutions across diverse professional disciplines. His work empowers professionals and institutions to integrate advanced AI into their workflows—enhancing productivity, driving innovation, and ensuring ethical decision-making. Eric's expertise bridges technical insight with immediate, real-world impact, making complex AI tools accessible and actionable for forward-thinking leaders.

Connect with Eric at **linkedin.com/in/prompttech.**